Phang Nga Bay. Paddle around a landscape filled with oddly shaped islands and hidden caves. See page 79.

Phanom Rung. This spectacular sanctuary is one of the highlights of the Khmer Culture Trail. See page 49.

Ko Samui. The place to swim, snorkel, windsurf, dine on the sand or just people-watch. See page 80.

Ayutthaya. A national treasure, this ruined city gives an insight into the ancient history of Thailand. See page 43.

Hill tribes. Trek by Jeep or on foot to see these followers of ancient rituals. See page 67.

Chao Phraya. Take a boat on Bangkok's majestic river. See page 37.

A PERFECT DAY

9.00am Breakfast

Drop in for a leisurely breakfast at The Verandah, on the Mandarin Oriental's riverside terrace. The luxurious surroundings make a fine start to the day, and there is the Oriental boat pier next door to whisk you on to the next leg of the day's journey.

12 noon Gold and dragons

Grab a taxi to Chinatown, which has some of the most historic shopping alleys in Bangkok. Along with gold, dragon dresses and Chinese lanterns, these lanes are full of cheap food stalls that make it an ideal stop for lunch. At Wat Traimit see the world's biggest solid gold Buddha.

10.00am Lying down

Take a Chao Phraya river boat to Tha Tien pier where, just beyond a market and Chinese shop houses, the grounds of Wat Pho house the Reclining Buddha. Afterwards, get pampered at the temple's traditional massage school.

2.00pm Shopping

A taxi to Pathumwan brings you to the heart of the city's mall district. As well as offering local and international fashions, Siam Paragon hosts Sea Life Ocean World, home to penguins, sharks, sting rays and other creatures of the deep.

IN BANGKOK

6.00pm **River sunset**

Hop on the Skytrain to Saphan Taksin station, from where it is a ten minute walk to the 200m (656ft) -high, al fresco rooftop restaurant Sirocco. Have a sunset cocktail at the rooftop bar with stunning views along the Chao Phraya River.

4.00pm **Culture**

A ten minute walk away, the Bangkok Art and Culture Centre has regular exhibitions by local and international artists, restaurants and a café. A further 15 minutes' walk away is Jim Thompson's House and Museum, a traditional Thai house full of artefacts. There's a café here, too.

10.30pm **Bars and clubs**

Take the Skytrain to Nana Station and stroll down Sukhumvit Soi 11, the location of two of Bangkok's best clubs. Q Bar has probably the best stocked bar in the city, with 50 brands of vodka alone, while Bed Supperclub has dining and floor shows as you lie on beds. Or try Cheap Charlie's. It's just a bar – no roof, no walls.

8.30pm **Night market**

Ten minutes in a taxi brings you to the infamous Patpong red light district, which has a bustling night market. The stalls are full of funky T-shirts, watches, jewellery, CDs and DVDs. Bargain hard. There's a good choice of restaurants and bars in the surrounding streets, with and without the infamous pole dancers and ping pong acrobatics.

CONTENTS

INTRODUCTION

As the only country in Southeast Asia that was never colonised, Thailand explodes with the boundless energy and self-confidence of its people. Literally translated, Thailand means 'Land of the Free', although it is most often referred to as 'Land of Smiles'. The Thais are easy-going and proud of their country. And they are always smiling. They value *jai yen* or a 'cool heart' and dislike hot tempers and loud voices. They are warm and welcoming to foreigners. Even on Bangkok's impossibly crowded streets, a visitor will feel quite safe asking a stranger for directions.

There is a sense of calm and tolerance that prevails throughout the country, perhaps due to the fact that over 90 percent of the population is Buddhist.

Founded in India, Buddhism first came to Thailand in 3BC, and thrived as the religion of kings and as a unifier of the people. Shrines, Buddha replicas and temples are found in abundance in

Buddhism is central to the Thai way of life

every city and village. The Buddhist philosophy permeates all facets of national life. Wherever you go, you will see monks with orange robes and shaven heads strolling the streets. Visit a temple and you may even witness an ordination ceremony when saffron-robed novices are carried high above the shoulders of their friends and families.

Members of a hill tribe near the town of Mae Sariang

Thailand and its attractions

Roughly the size of Texas or France, Thailand offers a vast variety of holiday possibilities. You'll find thick jungles, bustling cities and sparkling beach resorts. In the northern city of Chiang Mai, there is one of the world's most fascinating night markets. Those interested in purchasing silk, woven baskets and lacquered wood will want to shop here; it's also an excellent place to buy imitation designer-wear at incredibly low prices. In the lush valleys north of Chiang Mai you'll see the many orchid farms and elephant training camps that help give Thailand its unique identity.

Khao Yai National Park contains mostly tropical forest

Going deeper into the northern regions, to Chiang Rai and the Golden Triangle, hill-tribes follow rituals established thousands of years ago. Don't miss the opportunity to take a boat-trip down the Mekong, one of the world's great rivers. It runs down from Tibet, irrigating the rice fields in the north of Thailand, Laos and Cambodia before it empties out in the Mekong Delta of South Vietnam. If it's trekking in the jungles that you're after, then head further northwest, to the town of Mae Hong Son, deep in the jungle bordering Myanmar (Burma), where jeep tours and overnight camping trips can be arranged.

In the centre of the country there are tranquil rice fields stretching as far as the eye can see, and the magnificent ruins of Sukhothai and Ayutthaya. If you prefer more natural attractions, head for one of the vast national parks, which now constitute a huge 34,500 sq km (23,479 sq mile) portion of Thailand. Of particular note is Khao Yai National Park where iridescent kingfishers and orange-breasted, red-headed trogons flit beneath the shade of the leafy canopy. Gibbons and flying squirrels, elephants, black bears and possibly tigers dwell in these vast stretches of dense evergreen. You might catch a glimpse of any one of over 900 different species. Orchids grow in abundance, and there is a multitude of butterflies.

Thai customs

On being introduced, Thais will place both palms of their hands together under their chin in a traditional Wai greeting. The head is considered sacred in Buddhism; try not to touch anyone, even children, there.

In the south, in the Gulf of Thailand, and off the sandy shores of the Andaman Sea you'll find spectacular tropical islands jutting out of the shimmering blue water. The resorts of Phuket, Ko Phi Phi and Ko Samui attract sun-worshippers from around the world. Here, the beach is the main attraction and there are many world-class hotels and resorts to suit every taste and budget.

Many visitors begin their visit in Bangkok where direct flights from around the world arrive at the Bangkok International Airport. Thailand's capital is one of the most crowded cities in Asia. It has the majestic Chao Phraya (River of the Kings) and many criss-crossing canals. The old way of life still exists along the waterways and floating markets are still a sight to behold, but these days there are also endless traffic jams and scores of high-rise buildings. After the initial shock of Bangkok's polluted and chaotic streets, you will

The Phra Si Rattana chedi at Wat Phra Kaew in Bangkok

begin to discover the city's many splendid sights. From the glorious Temple of Dawn to the magnificent reclining Buddha and the impressive Grand Palace, Bangkok is rich in royal, religious and historical monuments. It has excellent shopping in its many malls and endless shop-lined streets.

With its diverse range of restaurants, the city is also a food-lover's paradise. Fresh, delicious and inexpensive food is found practically everywhere in this urban agglomeration of more than 14 million residents. But there are upmarket options, too. From simple street-side eateries to elegant dining rooms overlooking the Chao Phraya river, you will definitely eat well in Bangkok. Thai cooking is based on balancing foods between spicy, sour, hot and sweet; the success of any meal relies on creating delightful contrasts, which ensure that the palate never becomes jaded. Popular delicacies such as prawns in coconut, or succulent chicken wrapped in a banana leaf take their place among an array of hotter culinary specialities. With so much variety you could enjoy a different dish every day of your visit and leave with plenty of fine dishes still unsampled.

When to go

To some visitors, the climate can seem even more extreme than the food. Thailand's weather can appear to be hot, hotter and hottest. The hottest months are April and May when the country is at its driest before the rains arrive. June to October is the less hot monsoon season, when the rains come in heavy downpours, usually in the afternoons, but only lasting for an hour or two. November to February is the least hot period and inevitably forms the high tourist season in Thailand. Cool northern winds blow down from China, making Bangkok more tolerable for visitors. Northern regions can be chilly.

Although many travellers avoid the country during the monsoon months, this can actually be a very pleasant time to visit. Domestic flights are virtually empty and temples and beaches are not as crowded. If you don't mind the occasional rains, then you'll be rewarded with reduced hotel rates and restaurants eager to please the adventurous off-season traveller.

Boat navigating at a floating market

A warm welcome

In the final analysis, Thailand's people – even more than the sights, the scenery and the food – often afford the most memorable experiences. From friendly northerners who may sell you sweet honey pineapple by the side of the road to the smiling fishermen of the southern beaches, the philosophy underlying every aspect of life is, simply, *mai pen rai* ('no worries').

A BRIEF HISTORY

Archaeological finds in Ban Chiang, northeast Thailand, date back over 5,000 years, proving the country was home to one of the world's first Bronze Age civilisations. What happened to those prehistoric people is unknown.

As for the Thais today, they are descended from many ethnic groups. The Mon Dvaravati kingdom flourished in the west from the 6th to the 11th centuries, with Nakhon Pathom and Lopburi as major settlements. East of the Chao Phraya valley, the Khmer empire of Angkor, strongly influenced by Indian culture, and forerunner of present-day Cambodia, ruled as far north as Laos.

However, the group who gave their name to present day Thailand were the Tai, who migrated in several tribes from China's Yunnan region, probably starting in the 10th century.

Around AD1259, the kingdom of Lanna ('Land of a Million Rice Fields') was established in what is now northern Thailand. Chiang Rai was chosen as capital until King Mengrai spotted five white mice, two white *sambars* and two white barking deer beside the Ping River, and relocated to Chiang Mai.

Khmer heritage at Phimai, central Thailand

Mengrai ruled prosperously until the age of 80, when he was struck by lightning.

King Ramkamhaeng

The first great chapter of Thai history began with King Ramkamhaeng the Great, ruler of Sukhothai (founded in the 1230s) around 1280 to 1317. King Ramkamhaeng – renowned for legendary

Sukhothai, centre of a once powerful kingdom

exploits on elephants – nurtured a powerful kingdom that was a thriving centre for the arts. In its heyday, the kingdom stretched from Lampang in the north of Thailand to Vientiane, now part of Laos, and south towards the Malay Peninsula. Sukhothai contributed some of the finest examples of Thai sculpture, many of which can still be viewed in parts of the old city today.

After the death of King Ramkamhaeng, the kingdom's power declined. By the 15th century the city of Sukhothai was little more than a provincial town, and shortly afterwards it was abandoned altogether.

Ayutthaya

Established in 1350, Ayutthaya continued for over 400 years and earned a place as one of the East's greatest civilisations. Under King U-Thong and a succession of legendary monarchs, the kingdom expanded rapidly. Towards the end of the 14th century, the Khmers were driven out of vast areas of central and northern

Riding round the Unesco World Heritage Site of Ayutthaya

Thailand, and the people of Sukhothai were finally vanquished. In 1431 the capital at Angkor in Cambodia was sacked, and Ayutthaya's pre-eminence was established beyond question. It became a centre for trade between China, India and Europe.

In spite of the loss of several kings – some who were either cudgelled to death or poisoned – the people of Ayutthaya were, by all accounts, a happy lot, 'much given to pleasure and ryot' according to the observations of one 17th-century traveller. Opium was in quite abundant supply, and cohabitation and wife-swapping found many enthusiastic supporters.

Many foreign travellers who visited Ayutthaya during the 17th century were impressed by the size and opulence of the Siamese capital. Directors of the East India Company compared it favourably with London, estimating its population to be anything from 300,000 to 1 million. With palaces, canals and temples, the city acquired a justified reputation for being the most beautiful in southeast Asia.

European influence reached its zenith during the reign of King Narai (1656–88), when Siam was visited by ambassadors from as far away as the court of Louis XIV, along with explorers, zealous Jesuit missionaries and traders. One Greek adventurer, named Geraki Constantine Phaulkon, was even appointed the king's first minister, and acted as the principal go-between when diplomatic exchanges were held. But his apparent influence sparked jealousy. Shortly before the king died in 1688, at the time of a bloody revolt, Phaulkon was arrested and then executed. Following this incident, Thailand had almost no contact with the West for a period of 150 years.

Between the 15th and 18th centuries, the Thais fought innumerable battles against the neighbouring Burmese. In April 1767, the Burmese succeeded in capturing Ayutthaya, after a 14-month-long siege. They pillaged the city and vandalised every aspect of Thai culture and art. The sack of Ayutthaya, a great tragedy in Thai history, still casts a shadow over the national consciousness of the Thai people.

One survivor, a young general from Tak province, rallied the remnants of the Thai army and managed to expel the Burmese garrison. Ayutthaya had been almost totally destroyed, however, so Taksin – as he was known – founded a new capital at Thonburi, directly across the Chao Phraya river from what

Absolute rule

When it came to rhetorical flourishes, the monarchs of Ayutthaya in the 17th century took the biscuit. Any mortal who was so bold as to address the king was obliged to start as follows: 'High and mighty Lord of me, thy slave, I desire to take thy royal word and put it in my brain and on the top of my head.' Some who failed to follow this code of conduct were summarily chastised with bamboos. Others were buried alive in the cement walls surrounding the city.

has since become Bangkok. Though his father was actually Chinese – and a commoner at that – Taksin was crowned King of Thailand. He ruled until 1782, at which point he was dethroned on the grounds that he had gone mad.

From Thonburi to Bangkok

The death of Taksin saw the rise to power of the Chakri Dynasty, the greatest in Thai history, and the one that still occupies the throne today. Rama I, the first Chakri-dynasty king, immediately moved his capital from Thonburi to Bangkok – on the east bank of the river – saying that the new city would be larger and easier to defend. He then went on to defeat a number of marauding Burmese expeditions.

His son, Rama II, devoted himself to preserving Thai litera-ture, and produced a classic version of the Thai *Ramakien*, based on the epic Sanskrit poem, *Ramayana*. He also re-established

European impression of Ayutthaya in the 17th century

relations with the West, and still found time to sire 73 children by 38 mothers.

Although no less influential, Rama III (1824–51) is largely overlooked by historians. As a devout Buddhist he renovated some of Bangkok's finest temples, including Wat Arun and parts of Wat Pho. He also went on to introduce Western medicine to his country – including smallpox vaccinations – as well as arranging for American missionaries to visit the country; one of them brought the first printing press with Thai type.

Wat Arun, which was renovated by Rama III

Progressive monarchs

King Rama IV (1851–68), also known as King Mongkut, is loosely represented in the Hollywood film *The King and I*, which is deemed disrespectful and banned in Thailand. Thais worship Mongkut as one of their greatest and most progressive monarchs. He was a modern-minded scholar of languages and sciences, and was a monk for 27 years before taking the throne. During his reign commoners were allowed for the first time to set eyes on the King, waterways and roads were built, and laws passed to improve rights for women and children.

Mongkut was succeeded by Rama V, who became known as Chulalongkorn, or Lord of the White Elephant, and was one of the most popular and enlightened of the Chakri kings. During his 42-year reign, he abolished slavery and established a schooling system, the first post office and a national library.

He led his country literally as well as symbolically into the 20th century.

The World Wars

The effect of World War I was to propel Thailand out of isolation. In 1918, King Vajiravudh (Rama VI) dispatched troops to France to support the Allied cause. A likely explanation for his sympathies is that he was Cambridge-educated and had served for a time in the British army. Once the war was over, Siam became a member of the League of Nations.

Statue of King Rama VI

One legacy of Rama VI was the use of surnames by the Thai people. Prior to the war, family names were not used in Siam, but the king decreed that all his subjects should adopt one. Women were also encouraged to grow their hair long, and the game of football was even introduced, with a royal team.

The genteel world of Siam was rocked once more in 1932, when a group of army officers staged a bloodless revolution, which brought the monarchy's absolute supremacy to an end. The authorities of Siam (by then renamed Thailand) signed friendship agreements with the Japanese in 1940. The following year, the Japanese invaded Thailand, and the Thais – seeing further resistance as hopeless – entered World War II soon afterwards on the side of the Axis. It was at this time that the notorious Death Railway was built, with its bridge over the

River Kwai. Despite the fact that Thailand ended the war on the losing side, it was later allowed to join the United Nations due to a legal loophole in the original declaration of war.

Since 1932, continual political turbulence has beset Thailand. It has endured 12 successful coups and had over 60 prime ministers, although some have served several (shorter) terms. Only one has lasted the full term of five years. Ironically though, Thailand is deemed one of the most stable countries in the region. It sided with the US during the Vietnam War, and throughout its history it has remained resolutely monarchist and equally resolutely anti-communist.

Modern-day Thailand

Three anti-government uprisings, in 1973, 1976 and 1992, resulted in many civilian deaths. Following the king's intervention to calm the last crisis, stable, democratically elected governments endured for the next 14 years. Thailand saw rapid economic growth during the 1980s and 1990s, until a market crash in 1997 caused currency devaluation.

In 2001, Thaksin Shinawatra won a landslide election victory but proved controversial. He defended corruption charges, but

Sandwiches for democracy

The Thai history teems with military coups. Since the country's first coup d'état in 1932, there have been 12 successful coups, with the most recent one in May 2014 being the first in the social media age. With the regime taking a very tough stance on the opposition, even liking an anti-coup page on Facebook constituted a criminal offence. As a symbol of resistance, the anti-coup protest movement used a three-finger salute. Once the military government announced that it would arrest anyone who used it, the protesters adopted a new sign of rebellion – a sandwich. 'Sandwiches for democracy' were handed out in the streets.

was condemned for suppressing the media and for hundreds of deaths in his War on Drugs. In 2005, anti-Thaksin demonstrators adopted the colour yellow to show allegiance to the monarchy, becoming known as the Yellow Shirts. The movement intensified after Thaksin sold his telecommunications company and paid no tax. In 2006, he was ousted in a military coup.

A Thaksin proxy, the People Power Party (PPP) won the 2007 general election, but was disbanded by the courts. Democrat Abhisit Vejjajiva became prime minister. Thaksin's followers, the Red Shirts, clashed with the army in 2010. 91 people died.

2011 saw the general election victory of the pro-Thaksin Pheu Thai party, with Thaksin's sister Yingluck Shinawatra becoming prime minister. But in 2013, massive anti-government rallies were held and the house of representatives was dissolved. New elections were declared invalid by the Constitutional Court, which also removed Shinawatra from office over nepotism allegations.

Amidst political turmoil, in May 2014, the army seized power in a coup. The new regime took control of the media, while martial law and curfews were imposed nationwide (although soon lifted). The coup leader, General Prayuth Chan-ocha, was made prime minister a few months later, and King Bhumibol Adulyadej endorsed his rule.

Guard on duty at the Grand Palace

The post-coup military regime (which remained in power at the time of writing) has employed stringent measures to crack down on any dissent. Unlike previous coups, a quick return to civilian rule has not been declared.

Historical landmarks

1st–11th century AD The Dvavarati culture flourishes.

7–11th century The Khmers rule large parts of the region.

1238 Sukhothai kingdom is established.

circa 1290 Rise of the Lanna kingdom in the north under King Mengrai.

1351 The kingdom of Ayutthaya is founded on the central plains.

1431 Ayutthaya conquers the Khmer empire centred on Angkor.

1767 Ayutthaya is invaded by the old enemy, Burma. General Taksin escapes and is crowned king the following year in Thonburi.

1782 In the new capital Bangkok, General Chao Phaya Chakri proclaims himself Rama I, the first king of the Chakri dynasty.

1851–68 King Mongkut (Rama IV) ascends the throne.

1868–1910 Chulalongkorn (Rama V) continues his father's initiatives.

1910–25 Rama VI (Vajiravudh) concentrates on political reforms.

1932 After a military coup Siam becomes a constitutional monarchy.

1939 The country's name is changed to Thailand.

1945–73 During the Vietnam War, the USA uses Thailand as a base.

1973–92 Internal politics are dominated by power struggles between the generals and civilian politicians.

1992 Demonstrations following the election of General Suchinda are violently suppressed. The king intervenes, forcing Suchinda to resign.

2001 Thaksin Shinawatra becomes prime minister.

2004 The Asian tsunami strikes southern Thailand.

2006 A coup unseats Thaksin. The ongoing political crisis begins.

2007 A Thaksin proxy party wins election.

2008 Mass anti-government rallies. Opposition leader Abhisit Vejjajiva becomes prime minister.

2010 91 people killed as pro-Thaksin supporters clash with the army.

2011 Pro-Thaksin party wins election. Yingluck Shinawatra, sister of Thaksin, becomes head of government.

2014 Amidst political turmoil the army seizes power in a coup.

2015 Coup leader General Prayuth Chan-ocha continues his rule as prime minister; elections are unlikely until 2016.

WHERE TO GO

BANGKOK

Thailand's capital might well come as a shock to the senses, but there is plenty to see for anyone prepared to put up with the heat and confusion. King Rama I modelled **Bangkok ❶** after Ayutthaya, with canals that ringed the city and many magnificent temples. The temples are still beautiful attractions, along with palaces and historic buildings, but today the city has expanded beyond the old town into a bursting metropolis. It's a mix of huge shopping malls, bustling markets, sleepy canals, and, of course, the city's notorious nightlife.

The heat and the urban sprawl make it one of the world's least walkable cities, and aimless sauntering may result in nothing but a twisted ankle, for the pavement is chronically torn up. Three preferable options are to find yourself a taxi, a *tuk-tuk* (a three-wheeled passenger-carrying motor scooter) or a coach tour, which can be arranged in any hotel. There are also two mass transit systems – called the Metro or subway (an underground network) and Skytrain (an elevated service) – which enable you to circumnavigate the city in air-conditioned comfort. Both operate frequently between key points such as Hualamphong Station, Silom Road, Sukhumvit Road and the hotels by the river (see page 131).

City districts

The map included with this book will help greatly when you take on the unplanned chaos that is Bangkok. The city's sights are widely spread, with several major neighbourhoods vying for attention. Start your tour with the area called **Ko**

Gold statues at the Temple of the Emerald Buddha

Food stall in bustling Chinatown

Rattanakosin, which has the greatest monuments and is situated just a stone's throw from the Chao Phraya River. This is the original royal centre of the old city, and is home to the Wat Phra Kaew and Grand Palace complex (see page 28), as well as Wat Pho. North, within the old city, **Banglamphu** contains the famous backpacker area of Khao San Road, and beyond is **Dusit**, which developed as a royal enclave from the time of King Chulalongkorn. It has wide boulevards, European-influenced palace buildings and Dusit Zoo.

East of the old city, lively **Chinatown** has a profusion of entrepreneurs along Charoen Krung and Yaowarat Roads and the small lanes (sois) that cross between them. Walk along Sampeng Lane (Soi Wanit 1), the original 19th-century market, or **Soi Itsaranuphap** ❹ for shops that sell everything from Chinese lanterns and wigs to gold necklaces and street food.

Charoen Krung (also known as New Road) was the first paved road in Thailand. It leads south to **Bangrak**, one of the city's original centres for Western businesses. Several churches and embassies are situated between Charoen Krung and the river, as are now-faded examples of 19th century architecture and the Oriental Hotel, once the haunt of such luminaries as Joseph Conrad, Noel Coward and Somerset Maugham. The area is well supplied with gift shops and 'instant' tailors.

Running east from Charoen Krung, Silom Road contains the modern business district and **Patpong** ❽, the most famous of the city's red-light strips.

To the north, cinemas, restaurants and giant shopping malls populate **Pathumwan**, where **Siam Square**, a low-rise grid of streets, houses boutique designers fashionable with the young. Look out for the 30,000 marine creatures at **Sea Life Ocean World** (www.sealifebangkok.com) in Siam Paragon shopping centre (www.siamparagon.co.th), and Bangkok's branch of **Madame Tussaud's**, which opened in 2010 (www.madame tussauds.com/bangkok). **Erawan Shrine**, the city's most important spirit house, is on the corner of Ratchadamri Road and Ploenchit Road. It was built by the owners of the former Erawan Hotel following various mishaps. There have been no further incidents, and today a steady stream of the faithful arrive to offer flowers and carved wooden elephants to the resident spirits.

Khao San Road

Further east, Ploenchit Road becomes **Sukhumvit Road**, a busy shopping, entertainment and residential area. It has cheap beer bars aplenty, red light districts at Soi Nana and Soi Cowboy and several of Bangkok's best clubs.

Visiting tips

If visiting the Wat Phra Kaew and Grand Palace, make sure you allow at least a couple of hours and don't forget that respectful dress (no sleeveless T-shirts, low-cut tops, short skirts, shorts or flip-flops) is required and the guards at the main entrance vigorously enforce this dress code. For a small fee you can hire more modest clothing.

Wat Phra Kaew and Grand Palace Complex

If you have time for only one sight in Bangkok, make it the Wat Phra Kaew and Grand Palace complex (daily 8.30am–3.30pm; charge also covers Vimanmek, see page 34; tel: 0 2224 3273; www. palaces.thai.net), near Tha Chang pier. No temple so typifies Thai aesthetics as **Wat Phra Kaew ©**, the Temple of the Emerald Buddha. Its glittering surfaces and wealth of art make it one of Asia's architectural wonders.

Wat Phra Kaew was the first major complex to be built in Bangkok. As you enter the compound, you will encounter an imposing trio of structures to your left – the huge golden **Phra Si Rattana Chedi**, the **Phra Mondop** (Library of Buddhist Scriptures), and the **Prasat Phra Thep Bidom** (Royal Pantheon). Behind the Phra Mondop is a large sandstone model of Angkor Wat. Along the northern edge of the model, you will also find **Viharn Yot** (Prayer Hall), flanked by **Ho Phra Nak** (Royal Mausoleum) on the left and **Ho Phra Montien Tham** (Auxillary Library) on the right.

Next you will come to the **Chapel of the Emerald Buddha**, which was specially constructed to house the kingdom's most sacred image, the Emerald Buddha. Sitting high on a pedestal, the 66cm (26in) -tall jadeite image is surprisingly small, but the belief in its power is apparent from the pilgrims who prostrate themselves before it.

From Wat Phra Kaew, turn left into the adjacent **Grand Palace**, where the first building of note is the **Amarin Vinitchai Throne Hall**, which served as a royal residence for the first three kings of the Chakri dynasty: Rama I, II and III. Built during the reign of Rama I, the hall contains two thrones, the upper in the shape of a boat, the lower covered by a magnificent nine-tiered white canopy.

Next is the majestic **Chakri Maha Prasat** (Grand Palace Hall). It was built in 1882 by the internationally minded Rama V, and blends Asian and Italian Renaissance styles. The approach stairway and central balcony are of particular note. These are topped by a traditional roof, which rises in stages to three seven-tiered spires. Below the central spire stands a golden urn containing the ashes of the Chakri kings.

Further on the left, a pair of 200-year-old stone lions stand guard at the entrance to the **Dusit Maha Prasat** (Dusit Hall), where kings used to conduct state business. It is now the final resting place for deceased kings before they are cremated in the nearby Sanam Luang field.

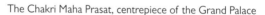

The Chakri Maha Prasat, centrepiece of the Grand Palace

On the edge of the square, near Dusit Hall, you will see a white marble building known as the **Arporn Phimok Prasat** (Disrobing Pavilion). Built to the height of the king's palanquin, this was where the king would alight from his carriage and adjust his ceremonial hat before entering the throne hall.

Opposite is the **Wat Phra Kaew Museum**, which has a collection of exquisite Buddha images made of crystal, silver, ivory and gold as well as some beautiful lacquer screens.

On the way out you can also visit the **Coins and Decorations Museum**. Displayed in glass cases in two jail-like enclaves are gold coins, swords and crown jewels, dating from the 11th century.

Six Great Wats

Visit six of Bangkok's *wats* – monasteries or temples – as part of your tour of its greatest architectural wonders. It is advisable to tackle these in two or more trips, as distances between them are considerable.

What's a wat?

You will see wats, or Buddhist temples, everywhere in Thailand. To help you find your way around, here's a brief rundown of the most common architectural terms:

bot: the main sanctuary of a temple, where religious rites are held

viharn: a replica of the bot that is used to keep Buddha images

prang: an ellipse-shaped stupa based on the corner tower of a Khmer temple and also housing images of the Buddha

chedi (stupa): the most venerated structure, a bell-like dome that originally enshrined relics of the Buddha, later of holy men and kings

mondop: wood or brick structure with pyramidal roof, built as a repository for a holy object

One of the best-known Thai landmarks, **Wat Arun** (Temple of Dawn; across from Tha Tien Pier; daily 8.30am–5.30pm; tel: 0 2891 2185; www.watarun.org), stands on the opposite bank of the Chao Phraya River in Thonburi, but is only a minute or two away by ferry. The temple was renovated during the first half of the 19th century by Rama II and Rama III, and is decorated with millions of fragments of porcelain arranged in the shape of flowers. The central tower

Reclining Buddha in Wat Pho, Bangkok's oldest temple

affords stunning views across the river. For quintessential sunset views, photographers should perch themselves at the riverside bar on the opposite bank.

Wat Pho ❸ (daily 8am–6.30pm; tel: 0 2226 0335; www. watpho.com), Bangkok's oldest temple, houses an incredible 19th-century gilt reclining Buddha in its vast white enclosure. Almost 15m (49ft) high and 46m (151ft) long, it reaches right up to the roof of the temple. On the feet, inlaid with mother-of-pearl, are the 108 auspicious characteristics of the Buddha.

Wat Suthat (Bamrung Muang Road; daily 8.30am–9pm; tel: 0 2221 4026, 0 2221 4331) was started by Rama I in 1807, but took three reigns to complete. Its 8-metre (26ft) -tall Buddha is one of the largest surviving from Sukhothai. Rama II himself is said to have carved the bot's teakwood doors. In the square outside, the Giant Swing is where young men at Brahmin New Year swung to great heights in a gondola to catch purses of gold hanging from poles. The ceremony was

The Buddha at Wat Traimit,
Thailand's largest gold image

banned in 1931 after several accidents.

The **Golden Mount** (daily 8am–5.30pm; tel: 0 2621 2280), accessed via Wat Saket (Boriphat Road; daily 5am–9pm; free), can be seen long before you reach it. It sits atop Bangkok's only hill – and an artificial one at that – surmounted by a big gold *chedi* (stupa). Spiral steps up the mount's reinforced sides lead to a viewing platform. Take a map with you to identify the palaces and temples spread out below the summit. The faithful make the climb for the shrine containing relics of the Buddha. These were given to King Rama V in 1897 by Lord Curzon, Viceroy of India.

The best time to visit **Wat Benjamabophit**, the Marble Temple (Rama V Road; daily 7am–6pm; tel: 0 2282 9311; www.watbencha.net), is at dawn, when the graceful marble is still tinged with orange and the monks are lining up for their daily alms. Built at the turn of the 20th century, it is one of the finest examples of recent temple architecture in the city. It is a haven of calm, with its inner courtyard surrounded by Buddha statues, and its ponds filled with fish and turtles, fed daily by the monks. Outside and past the canal are the monks' quarters, set among lawns.

The impressive Buddha at **Wat Traimit** (Traimit Road; daily 8am–5pm; tel: 0 2225 9775, 0 2623 1227; www.wat

traimitr-withayaram.com) might have remained concealed forever had it not been for workmen extending the port of Bangkok, who dropped the then stucco-covered statue from a crane, revealing the vast Buddha inside. This is Thailand's largest gold image, weighing 4.5 metric tonnes (5 tons) and dating from the Sukhothai period, when it was probably disguised to keep it out of the hands of the warring Burmese.

Museums and palaces

On Na Phra That Road, a short walk from the Grand Palace, stands the **National Museum** Ⓖ (Wed–Sun 9am–4pm; tel: 0 2224 1333). The museum houses Thailand's finest collection of antiquities. The sculpture, ceramics and jewellery exhibited offer an insight into the country's unique synthesis of different cultures – as well as the sheer variety of the kingdom's artefacts. Try to be there for a tour (ask at Tourism Authority offices for times) so as not to be overwhelmed by the museum's size and scope.

The exhibition divides Thai culture into several periods, starting off with the Dvaravati (6th–11th century AD), then tracing the development of political power to Lan Na, Sukhothai, Ayutthaya and ultimately Bangkok. The rooms are arranged in a chronological fashion, and you can see the changes in the portrayal of the Buddha, the overriding theme of Thai art, as you walk through.

The museum offers a range of other things to see, from an 18-metric tonne (20-ton) royal funeral chariot – which needed over 290 people to push it – to thrones, litters,

Museum highlight

The earliest works in the National Museum – from excavations at Ban Chiang in Northeast Thailand – are the most interesting: pots and jars with bold designs in the shape of fingerprints. The haunting patterns are curiously modern, and yet the pottery is probably 5,000 years old.

Jim Thompson House

19th-century Thai typewriters, and even a full-sized model elephant fitted out for battle.

A different sort of museum is situated in the tasteful **Jim Thompson House** ⓗ, located to the east of the city (Soi Kasemsan 2, off Rama I Road; daily 9am–5pm, guided tours only; tel: 0 2216 7368; www.jimthompsonhouse.com). Bringing a sense of calm to even the most frenetic of days, the cool timber rooms of this teak house are packed with priceless artefacts, sculptures and ceramics.

The story of Jim Thompson is as intriguing as his taste in art. A New York architect, he came to Southeast Asia as a secret agent in World War II. Settling in Bangkok after the war, he converted the Thai silk industry from a primitive craft into an international big business. In 1967 he vanished while on holiday in neighbouring Malaysia. The mystery of his disappearance is still unsolved. No trace of Thompson has ever been found, but this monument, 'the house on the *khlong*' (canal), is exactly as he left it.

Slightly south of the Thompson's House, on the corner of Rama I and Phaya Thai roads, is **Bangkok Art and Culture Centre** (Tue–Sun 10am–9am; free; www.bacc.or.th). Opened in 2008 in a state-of-the-art building with nine floors set around a circular atrium, it's home to various exhibitions, an auditorium, café and restaurants.

The huge palace **Vimanmek** ⓘ ('Celestial Residence'; Tue–Sun 9.30am–4.30pm; charge or free with Grand Palace entrance ticket – valid seven days, guided tours only; tel: 0 2628 6300; www.vimanmek.com), in Dusit Park off Ratchawithi Road, and built during King Chulalongkorn's reign, is reputedly the largest teak building in the world. It contains an impressive collection of objets d'art, paintings and royal jewellery, plus the first typewriter with Thai characters and the first bathtub and flushing toilet ever installed in Thailand. The palace has been restored under the patronage of Queen Sirikit.

One final building not to be missed is the **Suan Pakkad Palace** on Sri Ayutthaya Road (daily 9am–4pm, guided tours only; tel: 0 2245 4934; www.suanpakkad.com), near the Phaya Thai skytrain station. Suan Pakkad literally translates as 'lettuce garden', and this superb building is owned by Princess Chumbot and surrounded by leafy gardens. In the garden stands the delightful **Lacquer Pavilion**, which is believed to be the only house of its type to survive the sack of Ayutthaya in 1767. Bought in 1959, the pavilion was rebuilt here as a gift to the princess from her late husband. Some of the inside walls are covered with exquisite paintings – in gold leaf on black lacquer

Suan Pakkad Palace

– which illustrate scenes in the life of the Buddha and episodes from the national legend, the *Ramakien*.

Bangkok from the water

The most popular way of exploring the fascinating *khlong* (canals), which are so central to Bangkok's character, is to take either a tour from Tha Chang pier near the Grand Palace, or a similar trip arranged by any of the hotels. A one-hour tour is quite expensive, but will take you to sections of old Thonburi that you would hardly dream still existed – past floating restaurants, floating petrol stations, old wooden houses and temples.

Travelling by river boat on the khlongs

Most river tours leave early in the morning and include a visit to the **National Museum of Royal Barges** (daily 9am–5pm; tel: 0 2424 0004) in a shed in Khlong Bangkok Noi. The otherworldly ceremonial craft are trimmed with fanciful prows and elaborate red and gold decorations. The king's own boat is propelled by 50 oarsmen.

You can explore the canals on your own by means of the local boats, called hang yao. These long, narrow craft, powered by noisy truck engines, carry the propeller on the end of a long drive shaft – hence their name, which means 'long-tailed' boats. You can also hire your own *hang yao* by the hour, but be sure to agree on a price in advance.

Down Khlong Bangkok Noi (Small Canal) and Khlong Yai (Big Canal), handsome houses with gardens and fountains are squeezed cheek by jowl with old, wooden houses on stilts, shaded by palm trees. Nearby you will see rubber tyre factories next to temples, floating markets and snack bars.

If you prefer slower and cheaper transport, although it doesn't travel the *khlongs*, take the **Chao Phraya Tourist Boat** (operates daily 9.30am–4pm; tel: 0 2866 3163-4), which costs 150 *baht*. The route begins at Tha Sathorn and travels upriver to Tha Phra Athit, with stops at six major piers along the way. Boats leave every 30 minutes, and you can get off at any pier and pick up another boat later. You can use the ticket on the Chao Phraya River Express Boat 9.30am–7.30pm. The express boats travel between Tha Nonthaburi pier in the north and Tha Wat Rajsingkorn in the south, and between Pakkret, Nonthaburi and Sathorn.

Other sights

The **Queen Saovabha Memorial Institute** (Mon–Fri 9.30am–3.30pm, Sat–Sun and holidays 9.30am–1pm; tel: 0 2252 01614; www.saovabha.com), more popularly known as the **Snake Farm**, is oper-ated by the Red Cross. Its primary function is to pro-duce anti-venom serum to be used on snakebite vic-tims. Tourists may view the venom milking sessions, which take place from Mon-days to Fridays at 11am. Snake handling demon-strations are Mon–Fri at 2.30pm, and on Saturdays and Sundays at 11am.

Chao Praya river boat

Lumphini Park (daily 4.30am–9pm; free) is a haven of peace in the city centre. Thais come here to picnic, work out and practise tai chi. There is a lake with boats for hire, food stalls and a bar and restaurant at the park's northern exit from where you can watch the sun set. There are Sunday evening outdoor classical or jazz concerts from December to February.

Dusit Zoo (daily 8am–6pm; tel: 0 2282 71113; www.zoo thailand.org) was originally King Chulalongkorn's private botanical gardens. As well as 300 animal species, many of which are located around the edges of the grounds, the zoo has a lake, where you can hire pedaloes, and several places to eat. Thais come here to escape the city heat as much as to see the wildlife.

Off the centre, **Chatuchak Weekend Market** is a mind-boggling collection of stalls, where anything is available, from snakes to potted plants and herbal cures for insomnia. Chatuchak is open for sale of miscellaneous goods only on

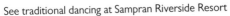

See traditional dancing at Sampran Riverside Resort

Saturdays and Sundays, Wed–Thu are dedicated to plants and flowers and Friday is a wholesale day (6am–6pm; www.chatuchak.org).

Further north from the market is the **Museum of Contemporary Art** (Tue–Fri 10am–5pm, Sat–Sun 11am–6pm; tel: 02 953 1005-7; www.mocabangkok.com).

Sanam Chan Palace

Also at Nakhon Pathom is the Sanam Chan Palace. This early 20th-century structure is in traditional Thai style, with the exception of one English Tudor building, which was once used as a setting for performances of Shakespeare plays.

Opened in 2012 and privately owned, it boasts an impressive collection of Thai modern art. It's well worth the trip.

EXCURSIONS FROM BANGKOK

The following excursions are all easily reached from Bangkok, and make rewarding side trips or useful stepping stones on the way north or south.

Rose Garden and Nakhon Pathom

One hour's drive to the west of Bangkok lies the cool and calm **Sampran Riverside Resort ❷** (tel: 0 3432 2544; www.sampranriverside.com). The 28-hectare (70-acre) property includes a hotel, restaurants, an organic farm and farmers' weekend market, as well as a Thai Village Cultural Centre. A cultural performance is staged here daily at 1pm and features folk and classical dances, sword fights, Thai boxing and a traditional Thai wedding. The resort also offers Thai arts and crafts workshops, farm tours and traditional cooking classes.

From Sampran, continue 30km (20 miles) west to **Nakhon Pathom** (widely believed to be Thailand's oldest town). This is home to **Phra Pathom Chedi** (daily 8am–5pm; tel: 0 3424 2143), the largest *chedi* (stupa) in the country, built by King

Mongkut in the middle of the 19th century on top of the ruins of an ancient temple. During the 1970s, this new *chedi* almost collapsed, but the Fine Arts Department took prompt action and fortunately saved the day, so that it can still be seen in all its glory.

Floating Market

You won't need a guide to show you the way to the floating market at **Damnoen Saduak** ❸ (daily 7am–11am), as everyone runs tours there nowadays. Even so, the diminutive boats, which are piled high with coconuts, bananas and durian, remain – almost – as authentic as ever. Try to get there quite early, while the women in broad-brimmed hats are still out in full force, paddling along the narrow canals and haggling over wares. Photographers might want to walk along the edge of the canal, or stop on the wooden bridges, which make excellent spots for observation. For a few hundred *baht*, a boat can even be arranged to paddle you out into the centre of the fray. At another tourist market onshore you can buy Burmese carpets, wood carvings and other such things. However, the goods are expensive, on the whole, and you will often find that identical goods are sold at keener prices in shops in Bangkok or in Chiang Mai's Night Market.

Traders at a floating market

Kanchanaburi

Its calm, lush setting on the banks of the **Kwai River** belies the history of **Kanchanaburi** ❹, for it was here during World War II that thousands of prisoners of war died building the famous **Bridge on the River Kwai**, as recounted in Pierre Boulle's novel and the film based on it. The current structure was rebuilt after the war, and only the eight curved sections on it are original. Two trains cross the bridge every day on their way to the town of **Nam Tok** (Waterfall), a pleasant hour's journey further to the west. You can walk across the bridge or view it from the long-tailed boats that hurtle up and down the river, stopping off at the cemetery and nearby caves.

Allied War Cemetery

To get an idea of the horrors of building the bridge, visit the two cemeteries, which contain graves and memorials to over 8,000 British, Dutch, Australian, Malaysian, Indian, Canadian, New Zealand and Burmese prisoners and conscripts who died during the railway's construction, along with around 100,000 Asian civilians. The inscriptions on the gravestones are as simple and moving as tragic poems.

Afterwards, you can visit the **Thailand-Burma Railway Centre** (daily 9am–5pm; tel: 0 3451 2751), which is next door to the cemetery. It has exhibits on the history of the Death Railway and even a full-scale replica of the original bridge.

JEATH War Museum (daily 8.30am–4.40pm; tel: 0 3451 5203) sits on the riverbank. Housed in a type of bamboo hut

Elephant trekking

used in the prison camps, the exhibition documents Japanese atrocities in photographs, paintings and relics. It also reveals the prisoners' ingenuity in surviving great hardships, as well as the sympathy and help secretly offered to the inmates by local people.

Sangkhlaburi

There are bases for tourists northwest of Kanchanaburi, making it easier to explore some of the most unspoilt scenery in the country. Some hotels pamper guests with air-conditioning and swimming pools, while a couple of others, slightly more spartan, are built on bamboo rafts floating in the stream. Jungle treks and excursions to waterfalls, caves, tribal villages and national parks, including **Erawan National Park** (daily 8am–4.30pm; tel: 0 3457 4222; www. dnp.go.th), can be arranged from these camps.

On the edge of Sai Yok National Park lies **Hellfire Pass**, christened by POWs who were forced to dig in this area by torchlight. The road to **Sangkhlaburi** ❺ runs between the densely forested mountain slopes of the national parks, passing Khao Laem Reservoir, with the town situated at the northern tip of the lake. Sangkhlaburi is an ideal base for elephant trekking expeditions to nearby Mon and Karen villages.

The **Three Pagodas Pass**, 12km (7.5 miles) further on, lies at an altitude of 1,400m (4,480ft). It owes its name to the three little white *chedis* erected here in the 18th century.

Ayutthaya

The most enjoyable way of visiting the ancient capital of Ayutthaya, 88km (55 miles) north of Bangkok, is by incorporating a trip on the Chao Phraya River. The River Sun Cruise (tel: 0 2266 9125, www.riversuncruise.co.th) organises daily trips to Ayutthaya, leaving at 8am by air-conditioned coach from the River City Shopping Complex and returning to the pier in front of it, by a converted rice barge. On the way you will see picturesque temples, rafts of floating logs bound for sawmills, and a countryside of rice fields and traditional stilt houses.

Before exploring the great historical site itself, most tours stop at the nearby royal estate of **Bang Pa-In** ❹ (daily 8am–4pm; tel: 0 3526 1044). This collection of palaces, set in gardens, was built by King Chulalongkorn in the late 19th century. The names of palaces like 'The Excellent and Shining

Bang Pa-In

Abode' and 'The Sage's Lookout' are as delightful as the structures themselves. Nothing beats the splendid **Aisawan Thipha-at** (The Divine Seat of Personal Freedom) in the middle of the lake by which King Chulalongkorn (Rama V) composed odes as the sun went down.

Back on the highway, continue 20km (12.5 miles) north to the town of **Ayutthaya**, former capital of Thailand and home to one of its greatest civilisations. In its heyday it was a fabulously wealthy, cosmopolitan city, until it was destroyed in 1767 by invading Burmese armies. Some sites are free to enter, others cost B30.

There are dozens of distinctive buildings, and you will be hard-pressed to visit the whole of the **Ayutthaya Historical Park ❼** (daily 8am–6pm) in one day. For a tour of the ruins, you could start at **Wat Phra Sri Sanphet ❹**, on Si Sanphet Road, near the tourist parking area. The temple was built in 1491 and once housed a 16m (52ft) Buddha image covered in gold. In 1767 the Burmese set fire to the statue in order to melt off the gold, destroying both temple and image. What you can see are restored *chedis* (stupas) which hold the ashes of King Borom Trai Lokanat and his two sons.

At **Wat Phra Ram ❺**, a graceful 14th-century building positioned amid reflecting pools, there is a beautiful cloister

Founding a dynasty

According to one of several Thai legends, the founder of Ayutthaya was the illegitimate son of a princess, who was discovered to be pregnant after eating an aubergine on which a gardener had relieved himself! U-Thong, or Prince of the Golden Crib as the son was named, became the first of 33 ruling kings, while the kingdom became the largest and most beautiful in the East as well as the principal kingdom in Siam for over four centuries.

lined with stone Buddha images, as well as several elephant gates, and mythical creatures called *naga* and *garuda*. The temple was built in 1369 by King Ramesuan, on the site where his father was cremated.

Next, visit **Wat Phra Mahathat** **C**, one of the most beautiful temple complexes in Ayutthaya. Once it held treasures of precious stones, gold and crystal, and a relic of the Lord Buddha in a gold casket, which is now housed in the National Museum in Bangkok (see page 33). Next to Wat Mahathat, **Wat Ratchaburana D** was built in the 15th century around

Wat Phra Mahathat

the tombs of Prince Ai and Prince Yo, brothers who slew each other in a tragic battle on elephant back. Rare frescoes remain in the crypt, but any portable antiquities were stolen or removed to museums years ago.

For an overview of Ayutthayan-style art, visit the **Chao Sam Phraya National Museum E** (Wed–Sun 9am–4pm; tel: 0 3524 1587), which holds well-preserved statues recovered from the ruins. There are beautiful bronze Buddhas dating from the 13th and 14th centuries, 17th- and 18th-century door panels with religious, traditional or floral carvings, and a hoard of 15th-century gold jewellery.

Finish off with a visit to the **elephant *kraal***, a few miles from town, where hunters used to drive large herds of up to

200 wild elephants into the stockade. Once captured, they were put into the king's service as fighters or, if they were the rare white type, as symbols of power. The last capture was in 1903 during the reign of King Chulalongkorn. If you want to learn more about elephants, visit non-profit organisation, **Elephantstay**, located in the village (www.elephantstay.com).

Ancient City

If your time is limited, there is no need to go to Sukhothai and Ayutthaya for ancient monuments. Loosely shaped like Thailand, the **Ancient City** ❽ or Muang Boran (daily 9am–7pm; tel: 0 2323 4094-9; www.ancientcitygroup.net), 33km (20 miles) southeast of Bangkok, has over 100 monuments, palaces, and other buildings placed approximately in their correct geographical location. Some are life-size reproductions of existing or lost structures, notably royal complexes from the ruins of Ayutthaya, others are relocated buildings that would otherwise have been demolished. The park also features exotic birds, monkeys and elephants. Travel agents run outings here, and there are daily buses from Bangkok.

Crocodile Farm and Zoo

Another 5km (3 miles) along the road from Ancient City is the **Samut Prakan Crocodile Farm & Zoo** (daily 8am–6pm; www.worldcrocodile.com). This huge enclosure is billed as the world's largest establishment of its kind, with the total 'croc' population put at almost 60,000. The farm preserves endangered species at the same time as it entertains and educates the public. There is also a zoo with exotic birds, tigers, ostriches and elephants, as well as a Dinosaur Museum.

Khao Yai National Park

Khao Yai ❾ (daily 6am–6pm; www.dnp.go.th) rises from the Khorat plateau northeast of Bangkok, baked dry in summer

Khao Yai National Park

and verdant after the rains. Khao Yai means 'big mountain', and the national park, located three hours' drive from Bangkok (200km/125 miles), is the oldest and one of the best in the land. The park can be reached by taking the bus from Bangkok to Pak Chong in Nakhon Ratchasima province, where there are pick-ups that leave for the main entrance.

The national park covers 2,100 sq km (837 sq miles). Within its boundaries are elephants and over 100 other species, including Asian wild dog, clouded leopard and black bear. Keep an eye out for some of Thailand's most significant bird concentrations, among which are some of the largest groups of hornbills in Southeast Asia, moustached barbets, orange-breasted and red-headed trogons and great slaty woodpeckers. Wildlife sightings are not consistently common or guaranteed, but the walks to waterfalls are pleasant. Night-time safaris employ spotlights to locate deer, tropical birds and – if you're lucky – tigers and bears.

Before being declared a national park in 1962, Khao Yai was known as a sanctuary not just for animals, but also as a popular hiding place for outlaws. This, of course, is no longer the case, and now the fringes of the park offer hotels, restaurants and 18-hole golf courses.

THAILAND'S 'KHMER CULTURE TRAIL'

About 250km (100 miles) from Bangkok is the provincial capital of Khorat, **Nakhon Ratchasima**. The richest and largest city in the northeast, it is a good jumping off point for excursions to the Khmer ruins of the Khorat Plateau, including Phimai, Phanom Rung and Prasat Muang Tam.

Khmer mythical lion guard

Phimai

Phimai ❿, 60km (37 miles) north of Nakhon Ratchasima, is known for its ancient religious compound at the end of the long, dusty main street. Probably built during King Suriyavarman I's reign in the 11th century, and situated not too far from the Cambodian border, Phimai was designed by Khmer architects, and predates Angkor Wat in Cambodia. Four gates dominate the ruins, the largest preceded by a bridge guarded by lions. Adorning the elegant arcades of the cloisters are intricate engravings of flowers, elephants and monkeys.

In the inner courtyard stand two small *prangs* (Prang Hin Daeng and Prang Phromathat), and in the centre there is an ornate dome with doors and a lintel, carved with scenes related to Mahayana Buddhism. In the gardens there is an open-air museum, with a collection of ancient friezes, statues and stone lintels showing Buddha, gods and monkeys.

Banyan tree

A pleasant way to round off the trip to Phimai is to visit the banyan tree, which stands 2km (1 mile) further down the road and is said to be the biggest in Thailand. Delicious Isaan food is served in its shade, but only in the dry season – during the wet season, the nearby reservoir floods the picnic ground. If spirits live in trees – as many Thais believe – then this prodigious banyan is surely thronged with ghosts.

Phanom Rung

Phimai may be the best-known and most easily accessible Khmer temple site in Northeast Thailand, but Buriram's **Prasat Hin Khao Phanom Rung** ⑪ (daily 6am–6pm) is better preserved, and set in more spectacular scenery atop an extinct volcano. Phanom Rung was constructed between the 10th and 13th centuries, but the greater part of the work was completed in the reign of King Suriyavarman II (1112–52), during the period when the architecture of Angkor reached its apogee. Today, after painstaking restoration, the sanctuary is the largest and best-preserved of all Thailand's Khmer monuments.

Phanom Rung was originally built as a Hindu temple honouring the deities Vishnu and Shiva. Beautifully carved representations of these two gods can be found in the lintels and pediments of the sanctuary. On the east portico of the antechamber to the main sanctuary you'll find a fine Nataraja, or Dancing Shiva figure.

Prasat Hin Phimai

Prasat Hin Muang Tam

About 8km (5 miles) south of Phanom Rung, in the dusty plain approaching the Cambodian frontier, stands the old Khmer sanctuary of **Prasat Hin Muang Tam** (daily 6am–6pm; www.muangtam.com). Fifteen years ago Muang Tam was a mass of stone walls and lintels, shrouded in dense vegetation. Today the temple complex has been splendidly restored by the Archaeological Commi-ssion of Thailand.

Other gems

Additional gems can be found in the neighbouring provinces of Surin and Si Saket. **Ban Pluang** (daily 7.30am–6pm), which dates from the second half of the 11th century and was once an important stop on the road between Angkor and Phimai, is a square sandstone tower built on a laterite platform. The surrounding moats and ponds have been turned into an attractive garden. Nearby **Sikhoraphum** (daily 8am–4.30pm) consists of five brick *prangs* on a square laterite platform surrounded by lily-filled ponds. The lintel and pillars of the central *prang* are beautifully carved with heavenly dancing girls, or *apsaras*, and other scenes from Hindu mythology.

Prasat Kamphaeng Yai

The 'Khmer Culture Trail' ends with the laterite sanctuary of **Prasat Kamphaeng Yai** (daily 8am–5pm). Here the ancient Khmer ruins rub shoulders with a much more recent Thai temple, and saffron-robed monks may be seen eating, studying or contemplating in the shade of the massive, attenuated *prangs*. Although the Khmer sanctuary was originally dedicated to the Hindu god Vishnu, the overall effect is most pleasing, and the active Buddhist presence strangely at one.

CENTRAL THAILAND

The most striking feature of the central region is its sheer fertile abundance. This vast plain that starts at Bangkok's outskirts is called the country's 'rice bowl', is home to one-third of the population, and the source of one of the world's biggest rice crops. Centuries ago, this agricultural heartland was also home to some of the kingdom's greatest civilisations, among them those of Si Satchanalai, Sukhothai and Lopburi, ancient cities that are as enchanting in ruins as they must have been in their heyday. Also in Central Thailand are two of

Rice cultivation

the country's most popular beach resorts – Pattaya and Hua Hin, located 147km (91 miles) southeast and 203km (126 miles) southwest of Bangkok respectively. Major towns to the north of Bangkok make good stopovers if you are en route to Thailand's northern region.

Pattaya

Visitors no longer come to **Pattaya** ⑫ for pristine beaches and tropical seas, for this infamous resort lost its original attractions to pollution and development many years ago.

It was in the 1960s that the provincial seaside town rose to prominence. This was when the first American servicemen arrived from Vietnam War duties for what was soon described as 'R & R' – rest and recreation. The Thais eventually realised Pattaya's commercial possibilities, and the area fast became a thriving international resort.

Nong Nooch Tropical Garden

Today, Pattaya is notorious for its sex industry, but has an abundance of accommodation, bars, clubs, attractions and outdoor activities that draw a mixed crowd, including a surprising number of families. The sea around Pattaya Bay is not recommended, so if swimming is what you are after, take a boat trip to the outlying coral islands. Or catch a bus to the beach at

Dolphin in Pattaya

Jomtien, a 15-minute trip south, where clean sand stretches for miles, with gleaming condominiums as a backdrop.

The adventurous can try out parasailing, sailing, jet-skiing and water-skiing, while others may prefer a day's deep-sea fishing, relishing the opportunity to try catching delicious snapper and sizeable marlin. Excursion boats take tourists to islands in the surrounding area for swimming and snorkelling.

At **Ko Larn** (about 45 minutes from Pattaya in a converted trawler or half the time in a speedboat) you can explore the underwater world in a glass-bottomed boat, gazing at vivid tropical fish and coral – albeit now sadly depleted. Many scuba expeditions begin here before going on to a couple of wrecks further south near Sattahip.

Land tours are just as easy to arrange. To the east, **Nong Nooch Tropical Garden** (daily 8am–6pm; tel: 0 3842 2958; www.nongnoochtropicalgarden.com), 18km (11 miles) away, features Thai cultural performances and elephant shows, and a vast acreage of exotic palms, orchids and cacti. Alternatively, try the water theme park **Pattaya Park** (daily 10am–7pm; charge; tel: 0 3825 12018; www.pattayapark.com), or **Pattaya**

Elephant Village (daily 10.30am–4pm, tel: 0 3824 9818; www.elephant-village-pattaya.com), where you can ride an elephant or arrange an elephant trek. For a strange cultural experience, visit Naklua's fantastic wood-carved **Sanctuary of Truth** (daily 8am–6pm; tel: 0 3836 7229; www.sanctuaryof truth.com), a 105m (340ft) -tall monument to Asian religions. It's made completely of hard woods with intricately hand-carved figures of gods and spirits. The sanctuary also offers activities such as speedboat rides on the adjacent lagoon, elephant trekking and horse riding, plus traditional dance and martial arts shows.

Pattaya offers abundant culinary delights. The restaurants serve first-rate seafood: there are plenty of simple waterfront restaurants that are rich in character but cheap in price. Those who prefer French fries and *bratwurst* shouldn't worry either.

Pattaya's nightlife, too, has something to satisfy almost all tastes, from big stage productions at Alangkarn Theatre (www.alangkarnthailand.com) and transvestite shows, to nightclubs, beer bars and all other establishments that have earned this area its reputation as the international entertain-ment resort of Thailand.

The beach at Ko Samet

The eastern seaboard

Further east of Pattaya, the small idyllic island of **Ko Samet** ⑬ has become a firm weekend favourite for Bangkok residents. The white sand beaches and clear blue water are part of a national marine park so most accom-modation is fairly low-key. The island is best avoided on public holidays, when visitors outnumber beds, and tents spring up everywhere.

Near the Cambodian border is Thailand's second-largest island, **Ko Chang** (Elephant Island), the dominant isle of over 50 that make up the national marine park of the same name. A current development drive is gradually transforming the hilly island from a place of backpacker bungalows to one consisting of higher-end boutique resorts, but it's still one of the most pristine islands in the Gulf of Thailand.

Snorkelling off Ko Chang

Hua Hin

There are quieter charms at **Hua Hin** ⑮, 203km (126 miles) southwest of Bangkok on the opposite shore of the Gulf of Thailand. A slew of condominiums and retirement homes are changing this former fishing village, and its long, sweeping beaches are no longer as pleasant as they once were for swimming. They do, however, make fine strolling ground, with watersports, deckchairs to laze in, and pony-riding. The surrounding area has plentiful golf courses and luxury spa retreats, while the pier restaurants on Thanon Naresdamri grill excellent seafood.

Lopburi

Lopburi's ⑯ dominant features are the superb stone temples built by the Khmers. These can be spotted even from the railway station, as can the French-style architecture and several hundred monkeys that have become this town's other lasting claim to fame.

Originally one of the capitals of the Khmer people, Lopburi flourished under Thai rule in the 17th century. King Narai chose the town as an alternative capital, in case some unforeseen fate befell Ayutthaya. His caution was justified: Ayutthaya was sacked by the Burmese the following century.

Begin your tour at **King Narai's Palace** or Phra Narai Ratchaniwet (Wed–Sun 8.30am–4.30pm; tel: 0 3641 1458), which was constructed in the mid-17th century, and took more than 12 years to complete. Inside is the National Museum, housing exquisite examples of Khmer art. The palace also incorporates the old treasure houses, a banquet hall, an audience hall for high-ranking foreign visitors and stables.

Stone temple resident in Lopburi

After the palace, visit **Ban Vichayen** (Wed–Sun 7am–5pm), which originally served as the residence of Chevalier de Chaumont, the first French ambassador to Thailand. Later it was the residence of Constantine Phaulkon (see page 17).

Near the railway station, **Wat Phra Si Rattana Mahathat** (Wed–Sun 7am–5pm) is a fine example of 12th-century Khmer-style architecture, with its *chedis* built in Sukhothai style.

Lopburi's famous monkeys can be found by the railway in the Kala Shrine, as well as in nearby **Phra Prang Sam Yot** (Wed–Sun 6am–6pm), a magnificent 13th-century temple with three distinctive *prangs* from which they like to hang, begging food from visitors. Keep firm hold of

Reaching Sukhothai

The Sukhothai ruins lie within the boundaries of the historical park, 13km (8 miles) west of the new town of Sukhothai, and are reached easily by *songthaew*, pick-up trucks with seats in the back, which carry as many passengers as can be squeezed in.

your camera and other valuables, as monkeys clutching stolen goods are a not uncommon sight.

Sukhothai

Sukhothai ⑰, the most striking of Thailand's various spectacular ruined cities, lies 427km (265 miles) north of Bangkok, surrounded by rice fields and distant hills. Built in the mid 13th and early 14th centuries under the legendary King Ramkam-haeng, Sukhothai flourished for almost 150 years until vanquished by Ayutthaya, and its people fled. Until around 40 years ago, the ancient capital was hidden by jungle, the outlines of the classical towers camouflaged by heavy undergrowth. The situation is now better, for in a huge renovation programme implemented by Unesco and Thailand's government, some 200 moats, kilns, images and temples have been partially restored to the glory of earlier days.

For a glimpse of some remarkable sculptures, start at the **Ramkamhaeng National Museum** (daily 9am–4pm; tel: 0 5561 2167), near the Kamphaeng Hek Gate. This houses a splendid 14th-century example of the Walking Buddha, which is, according to archaeologists, the finest of all Thai Buddhas. A replica of King Ramkamhaeng's famous inscription is also on show. This oft-repeated quotation is the earliest example of Thai script and includes the words: 'In the water there are fish, in the fields there is rice… those who choose to laugh, laugh, those who choose to cry, cry.'

A short walk across the **Sukhothai Historical Park** (daily 6am–9pm, tickets sold until 6pm) past the moat brings you to **Wat Mahathat**, the Temple of the Great Relic. This is Sukhothai's biggest and finest temple, dating from the 13th century and housing rows of the standing Buddha images known as Phra Attharot.

Continue by visiting beautiful **Wat Sa Si** (Temple of the Splendid Pond), with its graceful image of the walking Buddha and slender *chedi* shaped like a bell, and **Wat Trapang Ngoen**, situated around a large lake which floods occasionally during the rainy season. Carry on to the west outside the walled city and you reach **Wat Si Chum**, with its massive seated Buddha measuring 15m (49ft) from knee to knee, and each finger the size of a person. The sanctuary walls are 3m (10ft) thick and contain a secret passage off to the left just inside the entrance. This passage was used by the king, though for what purpose is not clear.

Loi Krathong

The best time of year to visit Sukhothai is on the full moon of the 12th lunar month (mid-November), when Thailand's most beautiful and serene festival, known as Loi Krathong, is celebrated. It is believed to have started here some 700 years ago, after one of the king's concubines fashioned a lantern from carved fruit and sent it floating down the river bearing a lighted candle. Now, thousands of people gather by water all over the country to launch boats made of banana leaves to celebrate the end of the rainy season. Sukhothai has colourful processions and a display of fireworks.

The temple of **Wat Saphan Hin**, 2km (1 mile) west of the city, is known as the Temple of the Stone Bridge, after the slate pathway leading up the hill. It is a long haul to the summit, on which stands a Buddha statue more than 12m (40ft) tall. However, it is a trip that is well worth the effort.

Si Satchanalai

If you still have a craving for more temples, you may like to consider making an afternoon's excursion to the **Si Satchanalai Historical Park** (daily 6am–9pm), 55km (34 miles) to the north of Sukhothai. Si Satchanalai is the sister city of Sukhothai,

The massive Buddha at Wat Si Chum, Sukhothai

but is wilder and less visited by tourists, with ramshackle temples and an air of faded grandeur. At the top of a steep flight of steps is the ruined **Wat Khao Suwan Khiri**, which is worth the climb for the views alone.

Hire a bicycle at the entrance to the historical park and explore what many regard as the city's most impressive temple, **Wat Chang Lom** (which translates literally as 'Temple Surrounded by Elephants'). The *chedi* is surrounded by 39 standing elephants and has a stairway representing a ladder to heaven. Real elephants can usually be found in front of the temple, and should you wish to, it is often possible to get rides around the park.

The Si Satchanalai area was the centre of a ceramics industry during the Sukhothai period. In nearby **Ban Ko Noi**, a village 4km (2.5 miles) to the north, archaeologists have discovered kilns that might revolutionise historical thinking by proving that the Thais began producing pottery 400 years earlier than the Chinese.

Phitsanulok

A wide river cuts through the heart of Phitsanulok, about 390km (240 miles) to the north of Bangkok, separating the old part of town into two. Although the broad banks of the River Nan can make a pleasant spot to rest, the real

Chinarat Buddha in Wat Phra Si Rattana Mahathat

attraction is **Wat Phra Si Rattana Mahathat** (temple daily 6.30am–6.30pm, antique museum Wed–Sun 9am–4pm).

Believers have been coming here for centuries, praying in front of the renowned golden Chinarat Buddha, famous for its curative powers. The temple, with lovely mother-of-pearl doors from King Boromkot, was built in 1357, and its shrine is so popular that Thai tourists swarm here every day. To meet this demand, a variety of shops in the complex stock pendants, relics and other souvenirs. Apart from Wat Phra Si Rattana Mahathat, there are few reminders of the town's great history. A giant fire destroyed most of the old town several years ago, and now it is best known for comfortable hotels and as a base for Sukhothai excursions.

NORTHERN THAILAND

Stretching up to the borders with Myanmar (formerly Burma) and Laos, and following the line of the great Mekong River, northern Thailand incorporates some of the most beautiful scenery in the country. This region was once divided into small principalities, which were isolated by the rugged terrain and accessible only by elephant. Even today, the people of the region speak a distinctive dialect – influenced by Burmese and Laotian – and retain their own culinary specialities.

Getting there for today's visitor, however, is a simpler process. Thai Airways International flies to Chiang Mai in less than an hour from Bangkok, while air-conditioned express buses make the run in about nine hours, and overnight express trains in 12 to 14 hours. On a five-day visit, it is easily possible to explore the area around Chiang Mai and Chiang Rai – and even take a trek among the northern hill tribes.

Chiang Mai

The capital of the north, **Chiang Mai** ⑱, rises from the banks of the Ping River, bedecked with dazzling flowers, notably orchid blossoms, in the spring. Formerly no more than a hillside Shangri-la, the town has grown rapidly to become both a tourist magnet and a major city in its own right – with

Orchids

Some of Thailand's remote areas are happy breeding grounds for over 1,300 different varieties of orchid, ranging from the famous *Paphiopedium ascocenda* to the elegant 'Miss Udorn Sunshine'. The best place to see them is at the orchid farms in the area around Chiang Mai, although you only need to look in markets throughout the country to see and appreciate the kingdom's favourite flower.

Street scene in Chiang Mai, the capital of the north

the traffic and pollution to match. Several thousand luxury rooms and cheap, cheerful guesthouses are available, as well as European-style bars and restaurants. Tour operators offer countless trips to colourful handicraft villages, hillside temples and mountain tribes.

After the oppressive heat of Bangkok, the more temperate climate of Chiang Mai comes as a relief. The cooler weather is immediately evident (remember to pack a jumper if you are here between October and January), and so too is the abundance of fruit, vegetables and flowers, which can be seen at almost any time of year.

Chiang Mai means 'New Town' and was founded by King Mengrai the Great at the end of the 13th century. According to one legend, the city wall – parts of which can still be seen – was built by 90,000 men working in shifts round-the-clock. Mengrai also built various temples and fine buildings, some of which remain and can be explored on foot or by hiring a bicycle or motorbike. Don't forget to go to the handicraft centres nearby for silk, painted umbrellas and lacquerware.

Inside the city

Start your tour at **Wat Chiang Man** (daily 8am–5pm), within the old city walls. Built in the 13th century under King Mengrai, it contains two important religious statues, the Crystal and Marble Buddhas – protected behind a railing, bars and glass – which were ancient long before this monastery had been conceived. Sculpted elephants surround a *chedi* at the rear of the temple.

Walk south for 15 minutes and you reach the huge, ruined **Wat Chedi Luang** (daily 8am–5pm). Built in the 15th century, it was damaged during an earthquake over 400 years ago. In the temple grounds stands a gigantic gum tree shrouded in silk which, it is said, will continue to grow for as long as the city prospers. Beneath the tree, locals leave wooden elephants and phallic objects as offerings to the guardian spirit of the city.

Continue west to find **Wat Phra Singh** (daily 8am–5pm), home to a magnificent Buddha statue. According to legend, the icon was on its way to the king when the chariot carrying it broke down in front of the temple. Believing this to be a signal that the image wished to go no further, the people

Ho Trai (scripture library) of Wat Phra Singh

Stall at the Night Bazaar
in Chiang Mai

installed it without question, and there it has remained ever since, along with a beautiful library and several fine carvings and sculptures.

The best time of day to visit **Wat Suan Dok** (daily 8am–5pm), which is off Suthep Road on the city outskirts, is at sunset, when the *chedi* is bathed in soft light. The ashes of the kings of Lanna are housed within the temple, which is said to hold an important relic of the Buddha.

A final temple not to miss is **Wat Jet Yot** (daily 8am–5pm), also known as the Seven Peaks because of its seven *chedis*. Local guides say it was inspired by the great Mahabodhi Temple in India in 1455, during the reign of King Tilokaraja.

For visitors who desire other forms of entertainment, drop in at the **Chiang Mai City Arts and Cultural Centre** (Tue–Sun 8.30am–5pm; 0 5321 7793) for superb exhibits and interactive displays, or the **Old Chiang Mai Cultural Centre** (daily 7–9.30pm; charge includes dinner; tel: 0 5320 2993-5; www.oldchiangmai.com), a charming old northern-style house, with traditional Lanna dance and hill tribe demonstrations. Alternatively, explore markets like **Somphet** (Moonmuang Road), or busy **Warorot** (Wich-yanon Road), where you can try exquisite local delicacies. In the evening, don't miss the **Night Bazaar**, on Chang Klan Road, which offers northern handicrafts. You'll be overwhelmed by the sheer variety, which is probably greater here than at any other market in Thailand. Animal lovers could head to **Chiang Mai Zoo and Arboretum** (daily 8am–4.30pm; www.chiangmaizoo.com).

Outside the city

Explore the following temples, villages and other attractions as part of either a half-day tour or a more extended itinerary. At the **Chiang Dao Elephant Training Centre** (daily 8am–5pm, elephant training session at 10am; tel: 0 5329 8553; www.chiangdaoelephantcamp.com), 56km (35 miles) north from Chiang Mai, you can watch elephants timber-lifting and bathing in the river and then go elephant riding. Years ago, elephants were commonly used throughout the north for transport across inhospitable terrain and for dragging logs to the river, for floating downstream. Today, you can ride on one of the giants of the jungle, and then take a raft trip through the lush countryside.

Silk weaving

Wooden statues, huge clay pots and coloured paper umbrellas bedeck the road to the village of **San Kamphaeng**, 13km (8 miles) east of Chiang Mai, which is known as the handicrafts centre of northern Thailand. In the factories and warehouses, you can watch the locals as they weave silk from cocoons or make lacquerware or painted umbrellas. Purchases can be shipped home, and credit cards are widely accepted.

Some 16km (10 miles) northwest of Chiang Mai is the 1,600m (5,120ft) -high peak of **Doi Suthep**. There are magnificent bird's eye views of the city and the surroundings from the summit and just below lies the most famous temple in North Thailand, **Wat Phra That Doi Suthep** (daily 6am–5pm). According to legend, during the 14th century a sacred white elephant sought out the site for the foundation of the temple by trumpeting three times and kneeling in homage to the Buddha. From the car park,

Member of the Akha hill tribe, near Chiang Rai

it's a 300-step hike (or a comfortable funicular ride) to the central gold *chedi* at the top, with its royal bronze parasols at each corner. The cloister is lined with many important Buddha statues.

Continue another 4 km (2.5 miles) past the temple to reach the **Phuping Palace** (open when the royal family is absent, mid-March–Dec daily 8.30am–4.30pm, ticket office closed 11.30am–1pm; tel: 0 5322 3065; www.bhubingpalace.org), where the Thai king and queen often spend some of the winter. On weekends and holidays, if the royal family is not in residence, the grounds are opened to the public in a blaze of lavish floral displays.

Another attraction in the vicinity is the small Hmong or Meo village called **Doi Pui** ⑲. Since it is the most accessible of all Thailand's hill-tribe villages, you are unlikely to find much authenticity. Still, if you don't have time to go trekking, the village does give an idea of the hill tribes' way of life, and includes a visit to the opium museum. Children sell colourful costumes, tassled bags and primitive handicrafts.

Among the hill tribes

To see the tribes in a more authentic environment, go along with an **organised trek** into the hills. You will probably have to walk considerable distances and sleep on less than luxurious floors, but with the aid of a guide, you can still locate numerous Karen tribes, who believe in the spirits of the winds and the rains, or the Lahu people, the men wearing silver buckles and black turbans and the women in calf-length tunics with yellow or white embroidery.

Known as the *chao doi*, the hill tribes are nomadic peoples who have migrated from Tibet and southern China along various routes into Burma, Thailand and Laos. In all, there are some 550,000 people, divided into six tribes: the Karen, Hmong, Akha, Mien, Lisu and Lahu, each with its own distinct dress, language and culture.

Generally, they are highland dwellers who opt to live above 1,000m (3,280ft). They earn a living from foraging, slash-and-burn agriculture and raising domestic livestock such as chickens and black pigs. All intertribal trade is done by barter. Traditionally, the chao doi

Trekking agencies

It's always worth dropping in to the tourist office to check which are the reliable trekking companies, as they can change from month to month. Be sure to use a guide who can speak English and, if at all possible, the tribal tongue as well, since this will greatly add to the success of the trip.

have also shared a common mythology. They believe that they live on top of a dragon and that they have to keep the peace to ensure that it does not move.

Travel agencies in Chiang Mai operate excursions ranging from one-day trips to more rewarding three- and four-day expeditions. Don't expect too much originality, though – villagers may ask for payment for posing for photos. While some are friendly and seem to be pleased that their colourful bejewelled costumes and simple huts are a centre of attention, others have discarded just about every trace of their traditions, opting instead for jeans, T-shirts and cola.

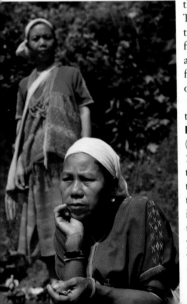

Members of the Karen tribe in a village near Mae Sariang

Lamphun

Although legend has it that the most beautiful women in Thailand are from Lamphun, this is not the only reason for coming to this peaceful, ancient town, which can be found 30km (18 miles) south of Chiang Mai.

A large monastery in the town centre called **Wat Phra That Haripunchai** (daily 6am–6pm; tel: 0 5351 1104; www.hariphunchai temple.org) is a busy educational and meditational institution. The huge, gold chedi in the middle of the monastery was begun over 1,000 years ago, and the workmen who erected it constructed their own simpler version outside the compound; it is now a ruin. Close by and built in modern style is the **Haripunchai National Museum** (Wed–Sun 8.30am–4pm; tel: 0 5351 1186), which has a collection of sculptures found in the Lamphun district, dating from the 10th to 12th century.

River ride

The most exciting way of arriving in Chiang Rai is not by the route through the hills, nor by the 45-minute flight, but by the least comfortable option of the riverboat from the town of Tha Ton. This is a trip for the adventurous – the boats are both small and narrow, with no toilets, while the engine is as loud (though not as powerful) as that of an aeroplane. Nonetheless, it is worth the effort – the views on the 4-hour journey are spectacular.

You can take a pedicab from the centre of Lamphun to **Wat Chama Devi** (or Kukut; daily 8am–6pm), a temple that owes its existence to Queen Chama Devi, said to have founded it when she ruled the Mon kingdom of Lamphun well over 1,000 years ago. Of the original elements, most memorable is a *chedi* rising in five tiers with 60 standing Buddha images in stucco around the sides.

Look out for the *lamyai* orchards that have helped to make this region famous throughout Thailand. This delicious fruit, which is known as 'longan' in English, resembles a lychee.

Lampang

Don't be surprised if you see a horse and carriage trundling down the main road of this beautiful old town, 100km (62 miles) southeast of Chiang Mai – this is a common form of transport in **Lampang ⑳**, and the best way to explore.

There are three temples here that deserve special mention. **Wat Phra Fang** (daily 8am–5pm) has a tall, golden *chedi* with seven small shrines around the base. **Wat Phra Kaew Don Tao** (daily 8am–5pm) reveals Burmese influence and has outstanding carvings. Considered by many to be northern Thailand's most attractive temple, **Wat Phra That Lampang Luang** (daily 8am–5pm), situated 18km (11 miles) from Lampang near the town of **Ko Kha**, is worth a visit for its museum and fine Buddha images.

Chiang Rai

Chiang Rai ㉑, a city located 180km (111 miles) north of Chiang Mai, is a good base for visiting nearby regional attractions. King Mengrai founded Chiang Rai in the 13th century, by chance so it is said. According to legend, his elephant ran off and took him to a spot on the Mae Kok River, where the scenery and military potential inspired him to build a town.

There are at least two temples worth a visit. At **Wat Phra Kaew** (daily 9am–5pm; tel: 0 5371 1385; www.watphrakaew-chiangrai.com), you can see a former home of the Emerald Buddha (see page 28), the country's most famous image. At the Burmese-style **Wat Doi Chom Thong** (daily 8am–5pm), you have the bonus of river views and a glimpse of the town's old quarter. Meanwhile, the **Hill Tribe Museum and Education Centre** (Mon–Fri 8.30am–6pm, Sat–Sun 10am–6pm; www.pdacr.org) sells ethnic handicrafts, with proceeds donated to hill tribe community projects.

Hill Tribe Museum, Chiang Rai

Travel agencies in Chiang Rai operate excursions to the famous hillside temple of **Doi Tung** (daily 8am–4.30pm), perched 1,800m (5,904ft) high. On the way you pass the former Queen

Mother's summer residence, an agricultural project sponsored by the Thai royal family designed to help hill tribes retain their distinctive traditions while integrating into contemporary life. The project encourages tribespeople to grow strawberries, cucumbers and cabbages, in lieu of opium. In return they receive government assistance in the form of schools and new roads.

Smaller tribal villages can still be found in the mountains north of Chiang Rai and the area around **Mae Chan**. Be warned, however: pigs, water buffalo and dogs may still wander picturesquely among the stilt houses, but

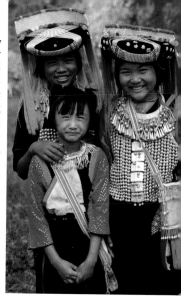

Lisu hill tribe girls at Mae Hong Son

modern life has not passed by unnoticed, and the children will ask for coins or, increasingly, notes. Even among the Yao villages of adobe huts with thatched roofs, many elders have learned a few English words. The women, in red-collared jackets and blue turbans, are usually more interested in selling handicrafts than telling of the Yao's origins in southern China more than 200 years ago.

Mae Sai and Chiang Saen

You can't go further north in Thailand than **Mae Sai**; beyond is the footbridge across the Sai River into Myanmar (Burma). This charming little backwater with a sprinkling

Mae Hong Son

of markets and guesthouses is a good lunchtime spot on the way to the Golden Triangle. Get there between 6am and 6pm and you'll see authorised travellers from Myanmar crossing the border into Thailand to sell products such as cheroots, packaged prunes, ivory carvings, lacquer boxes, oranges and, more discreetly, items such as gems and contraband cigarettes. In the market, take your pick from the wonderful Burmese puppets and tapestries known as *kalaga*, or pay your 10 baht to photograph children dressed in hill-tribe costume. These days it's possible to cross the bridge and visit the Burmese border town of Tachilek, but occasionally it is closed for security reasons.

From Mae Sai, tours usually continue the 12km (7.5 miles) to the infamous Golden Triangle, which forms a three-way border between Myanmar, Laos and Thailand. This spot once saw huge quantities of opium being sent across the border, destined for heroin traders overseas. Now the figure is dropping, as a result of government encouragement to diversify into less sinister crops. Poppies won't be seen here, since discretion confines cultivation to the less accessible valleys, as well as to those vast areas in Myanmar that are controlled by the so-called 'opium armies'.

A short drive southeast from **Ban Sop Ruak** will bring you to the friendly market town of **Chiang Saen**, set in a marvellous location on the banks of the Mekong River. Despite its dilapidated feel, this sleepy town has a remarkably grand history. From the 10th to 13th centuries it was the seat of power for one of the earliest northern principalities – traces of this glorious past are scattered throughout.

You can easily spend an afternoon exploring a moated city wall, the Wat Phra That Chom Kitti – reputed to house part of Lord Buddha's forehead – and the ruins of several other temples. Ten km (6 miles) north of Chiang Saen, the **Hall of Opium** (Tue–Sun 8.30am–4pm; tel: 0 5378 4444-6; www.maefahluang.org), set up by Mae Fah Luang Foundation, uses high-tech interactive displays to chronicle 5,000 years of the use and abuse of opiates. Visitors who have more time for leisurely travelling may also be rewarded with beautiful sunsets over the Mekong, and marvellous views of Laos, just a stone's throw away.

Mae Hong Son

December and January are the prime months to visit the town of **Mae Hong Son** ㉒, which lies between mountains 270km (167 miles) northwest of Chiang Mai and is reached by a hair-raising but staggeringly beautiful eight-hour road trip – or a less bumpy 30-minute flight. At this time of year, the sky is at its bluest, the winter flowers are in full blossom and the air is cool. It doesn't really matter which month you come, however, for this town offers no shortage of year-round attractions.

Burmese-style temple

Prior to 1831, when an expedition was sent here by the king of Chiang Mai in search of the rare white elephant, Mae Hong Son's history is as misty as its valleys. The expedition was so successful that a small settlement was founded, and by 1874 Mae Hong Son had become a provincial capital.

Although you're unlikely to see wild elephants, you will come across a number of Burmese-style temples around Mae Hong Son. They include **Wat Doi Kong Mu** (daily 8.30am–4.30pm), which looks down from the top of the 250m (820ft) -high Doi Kong Mu, and affords views across the green Mae Hong Son valley and towards the neighbouring Shan state. Most people like exploring the market at dawn – when hill-tribe people in traditional dress can sometimes be seen buying vegetables – before going on any one of a variety of tours. Guides arrange elephant-riding and river-rafting, or will drive you to tribal villages at the Burmese border.

Around Mae Hong Son you may see the Padaung, or 'long-necked people', with their collarbones compressed by brass coils stacked up 30cm (1ft) high to make their necks appear longer than normal. Legend has it that the tribe's ancestors were a female dragon and the wind god, and it was in imitation of the image of the dragon that the women took up the unusual tradition. Inevitably, the reality now is that this appearance is primarily designed to attract tourists.

On leaving Mae Hong Son, drivers and bus passengers could return to Chiang Mai on a circular route via Mae Sariang and Hot, so that towns visited previously are not repeated. On the return journey, the relaxed crossroads town of **Pai** ㉓, a valley hamlet surrounded by mountains, is a good base for trekking. It is also a firm favourite with backpackers, so has a slew of bars with live music.

SOUTHERN THAILAND

Southern Thailand, stretching thinly down to Malaysia, gives you a choice of seas. The considerably longer eastern coast is on the Gulf of Thailand, while the west is washed by the Andaman Sea. On both sides you'll find sensational beaches, while the land in between – full of rice fields, and coconut and rubber plantations – is as scenic as it is fertile.

Planes fly to Phuket, Ko Samui, and Krabi from Bangkok. Otherwise there are trains and buses, and the opportunity to explore several of the small, picturesque fishing villages along the way.

Sea Gypsies

Nearly 5,000 *Chao Lay*, or 'Sea Gypsies', have their home on the Andaman Sea. Most live in coastal shacks, between Ranong and Ko Tarutao, although the most famous, the Moken, lead a mainly nomadic life moving on boats between islands. They have no written language and their spoken languages are mainly related to Malay. The Chao Lay suffered relatively few casualties in the 2004 tsunami, and it is thought their intimacy with their environment enabled many to read the early warning signs in the sea's behaviour and flee to higher ground.

Phuket

The island of **Phuket** 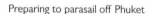 (pronounced 'poo-ket') is Thailand's most expensive beach destination, with beautiful beaches and luxurious hotels, in addition to sailing, nightlife and various family attractions. Covering around 810 sq km (313 sq miles) and made up of a mountainous interior, Phuket offers national parks, inland plantations and waterfalls and is the major departure point for diving in the Andaman Sea.

The island attracts over 10 million tourists every year – over16 times its total population – most of whom arrive by plane (55 minutes from Bangkok), although tourist coaches also make the trip in just over 14 hours, crossing the causeway from the mainland.

Although Phuket has been transformed by the invasion of tourists, and new hotels are almost as abundant as water

Preparing to parasail off Phuket

buffalo, you are nonetheless spoiled by some of the most beautiful scenery and clearest seas in the region.

From the airport, the highway south goes through a dusty village called **Thalang Ⓐ**, the site of the island's ancient capital. Burmese invaders besieged and pillaged Thalang in 1809. In an earlier and more positive chapter of history, the city managed to withstand a siege by the Burmese that lasted longer than a month. This battle, in 1785, led to both Lady Chan and her sister Lady Muk being regarded as heroines for taking command of the town's defence following the death of Lady Chan's husband, the governor. Statues of these short-haired women warriors stand on a roundabout.

The new capital, also called Phuket or **Phuket Town Ⓑ**, has a host of shopping centres, cafés and seafood restaurants, along with souvenir shops that sell seashells and locally cultivated – as well as counterfeit – pearls. **Jui Tui Temple** (daily 8am–5pm) is the centre of the annual October Vegetarian Festival, when people perform acts of self-mutilation, including piercing their cheeks with skewers. It is believed that thanks to these acts Chinese gods will protect them against evil.

Phuket Orchid Garden and Thai Village (daily 9am–5.30pm; tel: 0 7628 0226) has traditional dances, elephant shows and a handicraft centre, while on Yaowaraj Road, **Phuket Butterfly Garden and Insect World** (daily 9am–5pm; tel: 0 7621 0861; www.phuketbutterfly.com) has birds, tarantulas and scorpions.

Most visitors, however, find it hard to tear themselves away from the island's beaches. Water sports of all kinds are offered, from waterskiing to paragliding, and windsurfers, catamarans and yachts can be hired. Fresh seafood makes for memorable meals, and everyone at some stage treats themselves to the famous Phuket lobster, which is best eaten grilled and with a dash of lime.

Beaches and islands

The best beaches are on the western coast of the island, where fine, white sand slopes gently into the Andaman Sea (Indian Ocean). **Patong Beach** ⓒ, 15km (9 miles) west of Phuket Town by paved road, used to be the island's most beautiful, but has become over-developed, packed with bungalows, hotels, restaurants, bars, pubs and clubs. You'll also find the **Phuket Simon Cabaret** (daily showtime 6pm, 7.45pm and 9.30pm; tel: 0 7634 2011-5; www.phuket-simoncabaret.com) with its *kathoey*, or 'ladyboy' shows. From Patong, visitors can take a 45-minute longtail boat ride to **Freedom Beach**, located just around the headland.

North of Patong are the lovely **Bang Thao** and **Pansea** beaches, the latter home to the Amanpuri Hotel, one of the most exclusive addresses on the island. At **Kamala** beach, the popular **Phuket Fantasea** (theme park Fri–Wed 5.30–11.30pm, showtime 9pm; tel: 0 7638 5000; www.phuket-fantasea.com) has shows combining acrobatics, pyrotechnics and performing animals.

South of Patong, the wide beaches of **Kata** and **Karon** have an abundance of family resorts, while further south, at **Nai Harn**, is the sophisticated cliffside hideaway of The Royal Phuket Yacht Club.

It is possible to hire a Jeep to tour the island, but some roads are steep and accidents are not uncommon. The most dramatic viewpoint is the **Laem Promthep** ⓓ promontory.

The sea views from Phuket are dotted with 30 or so uninhabited islands, to which owners of long-tailed boats operate excursions for picnics and/or snorkelling. Scuba diving is first rate, either

Island escapes

Adventurers can escape the crowds by hiring boats to more distant, uninhabited islands – just make sure that before leaving you agree on the price and the number of islands that you will be visiting.

on live aboard or day boats, with plenty of coral and brilliantly hued fish. The most favoured diving destination is the **Similan Islands** , which have National Marine Park status. Deep-sea fishing expeditions can be arranged to catch mackerel, barracuda and sailfish.

Excursions from Phuket

Phuket travel agencies offer a variety of day-long excursions. Anyone who knows the James Bond film *The Man with the Golden Gun* will not want to miss visiting dramatic **Phang Nga Bay** ㉖, which contains the superb rock formations featured in

Phang Nga Bay

the film. Long-tailed boats skim through the mangrove into a dreamscape of mad mountain tops, and at two points of the journey sail through tunnels beneath limestone islands.

On the way they will stop at **Ko Panyi**, where the Muslim fishing people have built a village on stilts above the sea and now enjoy the attention of thousands of tourists, who buy their woodwork and fresh fish. The real highlight, though, is **Ko Tapu** (literally 'Nail Island'), which was formed thousands of years ago as a result of an earthquake. The island rises straight up out of the water to a height of 200m (656ft).

A separate excursion is offered to **Ko Phi Phi** ㉗, which consists of two islands, Phi Phi Don and Phi Phi Leh. Boats leave from Phuket daily and the trip south lasts two hours.

Day tours will take you to the Viking Cave and to beautiful Maya Bay. Underwater enthusiasts can explore some of the richest marine life to be found in the Andaman Sea. Fish are not the only attraction either, for high up in the sea cliffs live a vast number of sea swallows. The nests that the birds build so industriously at great heights are collected at considerable risk to the islanders – it's a profitable export business, supplying Chinese restaurants with the raw material for that expensive delicacy of bird's-nest soup. Locals believe that the soup will cure skin and lung problems as well as impotence and loss of appetite. Such is the demand that some nests fetch prices as high as US$1,000 each.

Ko Samui

Backpackers long ago thought that they could keep **Ko Samui** ㉘ secret. However, this palm-fringed island, just three hours

The famous backpacker island of Ko Samui

from the busy seaport town of Surat Thani, has become one of the best-known havens in the south, with idyllic accommodation and even an airport. Not that it has necessarily spoilt the laid-back feel of the place, for people are still coming here to laze on the beaches, eat excellent seafood and be pampered at one of the sumptuous spas.

The bow of a long tail by Phi Phi Don

Honeymooners and comfort seekers often stay on **Chaweng Beach**, which is arguably the most beautiful stretch, although packed with restaurants and discos. If you want something more chilled, head to **Bo Phut, Maenam** and **Choeng Mon** beaches. For cheaper accommodation, head for the south.

A plethora of beach sports are offered, as well as tennis, waterfall trips and even an excursion to a coconut-picking farm. For an afternoon diversion, you can hire a motor-cycle or Jeep to tour the island. The road follows the coast almost all the way round, though you should stop off at **Lamai** to see the erotic rock formations known to all as 'grandfather' and 'grandmother' rocks. Remember that the roads here are steep – and tourists with grazed knees are a fairly common sight. A safer means of transport is a *songthaew* (covered pickup truck with seats), which run almost 24 hours.

Beyond Samui

Samui is the largest island in an archipelago of 80 islands that also includes the party haven of Ko Pha Ngan, the dive mecca of Ko Tao, and the stunning uninhabited ruggedness of Ang Thong National Marine Park. Ferries and speed boats shuttle visitors daily between the various shorelines, with Ko Pha Ngan being the closest.

Geared more toward backpackers than luxe travellers, **Ko Pha Ngan** is best known for its legendary **Full Moon Party** on **Hat Rin** beach. Attracting thousands of revellers each month, the party is synonymous with drug taking, despite local authorities attempting to stem the narco-consumption.

Far more tranquil is a day tour of the 40 wild islets and lagoons that comprise the beautiful **Ang Thong National Marine Park** (www.angthongmarinepark.com), which inspired the fictitious island paradise in Alex Garland's 1996 novel *The Beach*. Further north is **Ko Tao** (Turtle Island), a small, pretty island with a relaxed atmosphere. Most visitors come here for the quality dive sites, with the numerous dive shops being the island's mainstay.

Divers off Ko Tao

Nakhon Si Thammarat
Thailand's most southerly provinces are plagued with Muslim separatist violence, and most governments warn against visiting Narathiwat, Yala, Pattani and Songkhla. This means fewer visitors to the area, and consequently the safe provinces are less developed and have plenty of

quiet beaches and a genuine local flavour.

Nakhon Si Thammarat's **National Museum** (daily 8am–5pm) has one of Thailand's most important historical collections outside Bangkok. The town is also home to the country's most famous maker and performer of nang thalung leather shadow puppets, and **Suchart Subsin's Shadow Puppet Workshop** (daily 8.30am–4.30pm; tel: 0 7534 6394) sells puppets and stages performances for a small donation.

Mermaid origins

Legends about seductive mermaids are believed to be based on sightings of the dugong, an inhabitant of the waters around Ko Tarutao. These strange mammals, related to the elephant, and dubbed the 'sea cow', roam the seas from Australia to East Africa, staying underwater for up to six minutes at a time. Hunters prize them for meat, oil, skin, bones and teeth, and despite them being legally protected, dugongs remain an endangered species.

Satun

While Satun Town's only real attraction is **Satun National Museum** (Wed–Sun 9am–4pm; tel: 0 7472 3140) and its Muslim lifestyle exhibitions, offshore lies **Ko Tarutao Marine National Park ㉙** (mid-Nov–mid-May). Consisting of 51 islands, it has Thailand's best coral reefs and is believed to harbour 25 percent of the world's tropical fish species. Wildlife includes whales, dolphins and dugongs, while the largest island, Ko Tarutao, offers hiking and cave exploring. The park headquarters have basic accommodation. In the 1930s and 40s Thai prisoners were exiled to Ko Tarutao, and in 2002 a series of the American reality TV show Survivor was filmed here.

Some 50km (30 miles) west, there are good dive spots at Ko Rawi, Ko Yang and Ko Hin Sorn.

WHAT TO DO

Thailand offers an unbeatable choice of indoor and outdoor activities, even if the heat is such that sometimes all you want is a swim. If you find you're lucky enough to be in Thailand at the time of a major festival, make sure that you don't miss one of the country's most joyous occasions.

SHOPPING

From the moment you reach Thailand you'll be astounded by the wealth of things to buy. Locally made items range from stunning silk products to wooden bowls and silver earrings, from clothing and fine woodwork to fragile, colourful pots. Whatever you are looking for you will find in **Bangkok. Pathumwan** is crammed with large, modern shopping malls and department stores where there is no shortage of either imported or local offerings.

Nor is Bangkok the only option. **Chiang Mai** is renowned for its handicrafts, while even the smaller towns in the northeast of the country offer many of their own specialities. In **Phuket**, the main Airport-Phuket highway has a good selection of handicrafts, while Chaweng at Samui is awash with typical tourist gear.

Remember that bargaining is the rule just about everywhere, apart from supermarkets and hotels – with even the large, upmarket boutiques occasionally being amenable to a little bit of negotiation. But do keep in mind that fixed-price shops may sometimes be no more expensive, and they come with the added bonus of some form of guarantee. A word of caution: only buy jewellery from reputable shops.

Wicker baskets for sticky rice, found in the northeast

Bangkok's Chatuchak Weekend Market

Markets and bazaars

Air-conditioned shops might sound like the best idea in the big cities, but it is the local markets that offer the real bargains. They are definitely worth a visit, if only to see the crowds and experience the excitement. Don't forget to take a camera and to get there early, as the heat becomes oppressive by the middle of the day.

One of the most famous markets in Thailand is Chiang Mai's **Night Bazaar** (see page 64) where you can find quality silks, handicrafts, rugs and clothing for sale, among many other items. The market gets going at dusk and the vendors start packing up just before midnight.

In the capital there are several markets worth a visit. One of the biggest, most diverse and best-known markets in Bangkok is the **Chatuchak Weekend Market** (see page 38). Fruit, vegetables and spices all vie for space with food concoctions you've probably never come across before. As for take-home curios, you might like a brass temple bell, a carved buffalo horn, a hill-tribe embroidered garment, or some handmade silver jewellery. You'll also find a huge selection of vintage and trendy street-style clothing, plants, rare antiques, and funky home ware and furnishings.

Smaller groups of weekday stalls can be found at Chinatown, the Thieves' Market and Pahurat, all located within easy reach of one another. **Chinatown** is worth a visit simply for the sightseeing. The emphasis here is on goods with a Chinese flavour or origin. The **Thieves' Market** has a wide range of curios, some of them antique – but remember that you need an export certificate for genuine items. For sumptuous silks, clothing, cloth and delicate batiks, some real bargains are to be found in **Pahurat** market. Here, products from as far away as India and Malaysia are sold alongside local items.

Best buys
Antiques. If you qualify as an informed collector, then you'll find worthwhile objects from Thailand, Myanmar, China, Laos and Cambodia at the Thieves' Market, in smarter shops or in the provinces. Experts at the National Museum in Bangkok meet the public on both Sundays and Mondays, when they vouch for

The art of bargaining

Want a natty wooden elephant, a lurid leather bag or even a ride in a *tuk-tuk*? Then remember to bargain for it. First ask how much the price is. Then name a figure considerably lower and somewhat less than you are prepared to pay, and eventually aim to meet up in the middle. A few hints to help out: always check the prices on several stalls to get an idea of the real cost; don't be misled by sweet smiles and sob stories – and remember, at the end of the day, so long as you are happy with the price you've got a bargain.

the authenticity of works of art and antiquity. Export permission is required for taking genuine antiques out of the country.

Art. Paintings in several media by Thai artists, often on familiar rice paddy or temple-spire themes, are sold in galleries and shops all over the main towns. Temple stone rubbings on rice paper are another typical souvenir.

Bronze. A great Thai tradition, bronze is now used for tableware in addition to lamps, bells, candelabra and statues.

CDs and DVDs. While Thailand has made some effort to stamp out pirated music, movies and software, many market stalls still warily offer all the latest media releases. Buy at your own discretion.

Ceramics. A particular wood is used in the kilns to fire celadon, a distinctive Asian form of pottery with a delicate green glaze. Porcelain is also made in Thailand. Ming and Ching dynasty bowls and shards turn up, salvaged from the river at Ayutthaya and Sukhothai.

Fashion. Clothes to order – allegedly in 24 hours or less – can be a bargain, but try to give the tailor several days if you want a first-rate garment. Trousers, dresses, suits, shirts and bikinis can all be made to measure. Women's ready-to-wear shops often sell good cheap copies of current European fashions. The domestic fashion industry is also coming into its own, with lots of trendy boutiques in Bangkok malls and around Siam Square.

Images of Buddha

Taking images of Buddha, larger than 12 centimetres (4.7 inches), or goods featuring the Thai flag out of Thailand is prohibited, and the export of antiques is strictly controlled.

Furniture. Rattan and hardwood furniture pieces are often bargains and can be made to order. Bangkok and Chiang Mai have the best selections. With the ongoing success of teak farming and teak recycling, teak furniture has once again become a

Tribal crafts include miniature figures carved from wood

bargain in Thailand if you find the right places. Asian rose-wood is also a good buy.

Gems. Precious stones such as sapphires and rubies are mined here, while others are imported at favourable prices from Myanmar (Burma), India, Sri Lanka and other countries. Bangkok claims to be the world's top gem-cutting centre. Seek out a reputable shop and avoid unrealistic bargains: fakes are common.

Handicrafts. With great skill, patience and ingenuity, the artisans of Thailand produce an apparently endless variety of hand-crafted objects. Each region has its specialities.

Homeware. Contemporary Thai design has become extremely creative in recent years, with many designers infusing traditional crafts and materials with ultra-modern twists.

Jewellery. Thai designers tend towards traditional styles, but original designs can be ordered. Choose carefully where you shop: the establishments that cater to tour buses are generally more expensive because they often pay the travel agency a 20 percent kickback on what you spend. Thai costume jewellery can be a great bargain.

Lacquerware. Look out for pretty gold-and-black boxes in the shape of fantasy animals.

Nielloware. Black metal alloy inlaid on silver is an ancient craft now deployed on jewellery and trinkets.

Pottery. A typical Thai variety – *benjarong* ware – has a five-coloured design on a background of grey, white or black. You will also see patterned porcelain jars, plates and pots.

Thai silk and fabrics. Happy silkworms keep thousands of nimble weavers busy, hand and foot, in producing the famous, colourful Thai fabrics. Ranging from lightweight blouses to heavy bedspreads, the long-lasting fabrics live up to their worldwide reputation. Durable Thai cotton, most of which is factory-made, goes into ready-to-wear clothing,

Lacquerware in the form of vases

towels, some toys and tablecloths.

Umbrellas. All around Chiang Mai, locals make hand-painted parasols – to your own design, if you wish.

Wood carvings. Figurines, elephants and hippos, teak furniture, salad bowls and a variety of other knick-knacks are exquisitely carved from wood.

Wood carving

ENTERTAINMENT

Thai Dance, dance-drama and music

The highly stylised classical *khon* drama, based on the *Ramakien* epic, was performed solely at royal palaces for the privileged. In a *khon* performance, masks are donned for all roles except the three leads where heavy make-up and ornate costumes subdue the personality of the performers. The modern adaptations presented during dance shows are generally known as *lakhon* where no masks are worn and the movements are less stylised. The *lakhon chakri* is often performed at temple festivals and at shrines. The popular burlesque theatre, known as *likay*, is much coarser, and is interspersed with slapstick episodes. The entertaining transvestite shows always include several *likay*-type scenes. The shadow theatre known as *nang thalung* originated in the south of the country and is staged against a backlit white cloth screen. It is most commonly performed in South Thailand.

Classical Thai music can sound like a mishmash of contrasting tones without any pattern. To aficionados, it has a very distinct rhythm and plan. A classical *phipat* orchestra is made up of a single reed instrument, the oboe-like *phinai*, and a variety of percussion instruments.

The only places with regular traditional dance and theatre in Bangkok are **Sala Chalerm Krung** (tel: 0 2222 0434, www.sala chalermkrung.com), which hosts *khon* masked drama performances every Thursday and Friday at 7.30pm, and a few restaurants which host dinner shows. **Aksra Theatre King Power** (tel: 0 2680 9999, www.pullmanbangkokkingpower.com) has Thai and other Asian puppetry with cultural performances themed around events like cock-fighting and *muay thai*.

Nightlife

Mention Bangkok to anybody and the chances are they will talk about the city's nightlife. In recent years the city has welcomed a whole slew of stylish bars and clubs that are slowly helping the capital to distance itself from its salacious reputation. Lounge bars, fabulous roof-top bars and chic design-conscious clubs are all the rage now. Quality music has at last become a must, with bars hosting weekly DJ-driven theme nights and also pulling in big-name international DJs.

Bangkok's Q Bar, one of the city's best clubs

Officially, Bangkok is divided into three nightlife zones: Thanon Silom, Thanon Ratchadaphisek and Royal City Avenue (RCA), where venues with valid dance licences open until 2am. The rest should close by 1am. In reality police bribes are common and venues might stay open later. People must be over 20 to enter clubs and

Bed Supperclub in Bangkok

almost all require you to show ID. Carry a copy of your passport, rather than the original. Good clubs include **Q Bar** (34 Sukhumvit Soi 11, tel: 08 2308 3246, www.qbarbangkok.com) and **Bed Supperclub** (26 Sukhumvit Soi 11, tel: 0 2651 3537, www.bed supperclub.com), where – as the very name suggests – you can also dine and lie on beds.

On the live music front, there are interesting local performances at **Tawandaeng German Brewhouse** (462/1 Rama 3 Rd, tel: 0 2678 11146, www.tawandang.com), while rock and blues fans head for **Saxophone Pub** (3/8 Phaya Thai Rd, tel: 0 2246 5472, www.saxophonepub.com). For rock-bottom beers visit **Cheap Charlie's** (1 Sukhumvit Soi 11, tel: 0 2253 4648), a quirky bar with no roof or walls.

Chiang Mai has few clubs. **Boy Blues Bar** (Soi 6, Changklan Rd, Kalare Night Bazaar, http://boybluesbar.com) is the venue for Thai style blues played by local talented bands with jam sessions on Monday. Down on the Ping River there is more live

Advert on Soi Bangla in Patong, on the island of Phuket

music at the **Riverside Bar & Restaurant** (9–11 Charoenrat Rd, tel: 0 5324 3239, www.theriversidechiangmai. com).

Phuket is big on Irish bars like **Angus O'Toole** (516/20 Patak Rd, Hat Karon, tel: 0 7639 8262, www.otools-phuket.com) while the late night dance crowd is found at the **4U Skybar Nightclub** (Ban Kata, Kata Beach, tel: 08 4376 8272).

The go-go scene

Several thousand nightclubs and go-go bars throughout the country cater to every taste. Although they are aimed at males, women are usually welcome to come in for a drink and a look. Gay and straight bars are increasingly run in the same areas, particularly in Bangkok and Chiang Mai.

Upstairs bars are frequently a front for live sex shows. It is wise always to check the price before entering any Patpong bar. There are occasional attempts at rip-off prices; if so simply pay the bill and get in touch with the tourist police. Remember that go-go bar 'women' are not all female, and that Aids and venereal diseases are common.

Provincial nightlife is often calmer, though many towns have nightclubs with hostesses for hire, massage parlours and the like. In central Thailand, Pattaya has a comprehensive night-life comparable with Bangkok's. Down in the far south, Phuket outdoes all other seaside tourist towns with a highly concentrated entertainment zone in Patong Beach.

SPORTS

With some of the most beautiful waters in the Far East, it's little wonder that Thailand is a beach-lover's paradise. Once you have finished sunning yourself, there is no shortage of other activities. Boats and windsurfers are available for hire at beaches, as are pedal boats and jet skis.

Fishing has only been exploited recently as a sport in Thailand, but the Andaman Sea has good options, including night fishing for shark, with boats leaving from Phuket. Good catches of sailfish, marlin and shark have been also made from Pattaya, but if all you want is a day relaxing on deck with a rod to tempt smaller snapper, mackerel or parrotfish, that can easily be arranged as well.

Scuba diving is especially good around Ko Tao and the Similan Islands, but is available at most major resorts, including Pattaya, and lessons are also offered. Most dive operators have PADI Open Water certification courses for beginners to dive master, and day trips (or longer) with live-aboard facilities to the best sites. **Water-skiing, kite boarding** and **wakeboarding** fans are increasingly catered for at popular beaches. Away from the water, **golf** facilities are first rate in Bangkok, Hua Hin, Phuket and Pattaya, with several championship-standard courses available.

Thai boxing

Thai boxing (muay thai) is a violent sport that combines Western boxing with Eastern martial arts. As well as using gloved fists, these agile punchers and kickers battle it out with their elbows, knees and feet. Fights are held year-round at Lumphini and Ratchadamnoen stadiums in Bangkok and at festivals and fairs around the country, where many boys begin their careers as young as seven. Tourist areas like Bangkok, Chiang Mai and Phuket have exhibition bouts and gyms where you can learn the moves yourself.

Trekking in the northern mountains is gaining in popularity. Week-long treks usually include three meals a day and basic camping equipment. The best town from which to begin a trekking tour is Mae Hong Son, where countless tour agencies offer trips with licensed guides.

CHILDREN'S ACTIVITIES

Although children may not take to the heat well, the upsides are that Thais love kids and there is an increasing number of facilities available for family holidays. Chiang Mai has **Chiang Mai Zoo and Arboretum** (see page 65) and the **Maesa Elephant Camp** (daily 8am–4pm; tel: 0 5320 6247; www.maesaelephantcamp.com), 30km (19 miles) from the city, where kids can learn about and ride elephants. Animal options in Bangkok are **Sea Life Ocean World** (daily 10am–9pm; www.sealifebangkok.com) and **Dusit Zoo** (daily 8am–6pm; www.zoothailand.org), while **Dream World** (Mon–Fri 10am–5pm, Sat–Sun 10am–7pm; www.dreamworld.co.th) has roller coasters. Pattaya has elephant battles and lasers at **Alangkarn Theatre** (Thu–Tue, shows at 6pm; www.alangkarnthailand.com) and **Phuket Fantasea** (theme park Fri–Wed 5.30–11.30pm, showtime 9pm; www.phuket-fantasea.com) has a circus. One of the hottest newer attractions (and not only for kids) is the **Art in Paradise**, an interactive 3D gallery using optical illusion so posing visitors become part of the artwork. There are branches in Bangkok, Chiang Mai and Pattaya (www.artinparadise.co.th).

Kids will love Thailand's beaches

Calendar of events

Check precise dates before you leave as the timing of many festivals and events depends on the position of the sun or the moon.

Late January–early February Chinese New Year. Many Thais have Chinese ancestry, and this week-long Lunar New Year festival is always celebrated with much gusto.

February full moon Makha Puja. A nationwide Buddhist festival with candlelight processions around many temples.

Early February Flower carnival in Chiang Mai, with floats, parades and beauty contests.

13–15 April Songkran or Water Festival. Thai New Year is celebrated nationwide by throwing water at everybody in sight.

Early May Visaka Puja. This very important Buddhist holiday commemorates the Buddha with candlelight processions.

May The Royal Ploughing Ceremony in Bangkok. Just before the rainy season starts, the king presides over ceremonies to bring good rains to farmers.

May Bun Bang Fai (rocket) festival in the northeast. Fireworks light the sky to bring rain.

July full moon Asanha Puja. Candlelight processions at every temple in Thailand to celebrate Buddha's first sermon.

12 August Queen's Birthday. Also known as Mother's Day, this is a public holiday.

Early October Phuket Vegetarian Festival in Phuket Town. Chinese festival with male penitents piercing their bodies with knives and needles.

November full moon Thailand's most beautiful festival, Loi Krathong. Thais across the country launch small candle-laden floats on rivers and lakes (see page 58).

Late November River Kwai Historical Week in Kanchanaburi. A week-long festival to commemorate the events of World War II with memorial services and a sound-and-light show over the famous bridge.

5 December The king's birthday is celebrated in Bangkok with an elaborate parade on Ratchadamnoen Klang Avenue.

EATING OUT

Good food in Thailand is as ubiquitous as beaches – and often quite a lot hotter besides. If you don't like chillies, don't give up on the food. *Mai phet* (not hot), stressed at the time you order, can bring a delicious selection of cooler, more subtle flavours that may include any taste from the sweetness of coconut milk to the pungency of fresh lemon grass, garlic or nutmeg and the saltiness of fermented fish. Added to that are tropical fruits such as fresh pineapple, a little sugar, a pinch of coriander – and, of course, a lashing of culinary inspiration.

Kaeng mussaman curry

Every region has its own gastronomical specialities. Up in the north, a local sausage known as *naem* is popular. The northeast is famed for its *khao niaw* (sticky or glutinous rice), normally served as an accompaniment to barbecued meat, as well as *som tam*, a tasty hot salad that combines shredded green papaya with dried shrimp or black field crabs, lemon juice, garlic, fish sauce and chillies. The south produces numerous dishes that have been influenced by the Muslim style of cooking of the Malays and, of course, all kinds of seafood dishes, including crab, squid, shark, freshly cooked lobster and mussels. Don't worry if you have a sweet tooth – you're not likely to go hungry at all. Many Thai sweets are based

on rice flour, coconut milk, palm sugar and sticky rice, and just about all of them are delicious.

When and how to eat

Most Thais work all day, grab something quick for lunch and have an early dinner. But don't think that the Thai version of fast food is just a bland rice dish. A 'quick bite' often means a tasty dish (such as *pad thai*) of sautéed noodles with pork, shrimp or chicken and seasoned with tamarind juice, lime, basil, garlic and onion. Even breakfast for locals consists of dishes full of fresh herbs and spices, such as sweet curry soup with basil served with boiled rice noodles. Hotels rarely serve such traditional Thai breakfasts although they will direct you to a nearby restaurant that offers them.

Food vendors line the streets everywhere and sometimes it may seem as if everybody is eating or drinking at all hours. Some vendors operate from glass-fronted carts, others with just large pans on the ground. Communal tables and chairs will be nearby. Slightly more upmarket are *raan aharn* (food shops). Generally, top-end Thai restaurants have milder flavours, as they compromise for tourist palates. Bangkok boasts some of the finest restaurants in the world, including the ultra-traditional **Nahm** and the modern **Sra Bua**, conceptualised by Henrik Yde Andersen, whose Copenhagen restaurant Kiin Kiin is the only Michelin-starred Thai eatery.

Local markets teem with vendors selling food items such as nuts, dried meats and sweets. If you're feeling adventurous, skip the hotel breakfast and stroll through an open-air market sampling the various treats. At lunch it'll be too hot to have the Thai soups so opt for a salad and noodle dish. Plan on having your main meal in the early evening, just after sunset when the temperature drops.

Soup is traditionally eaten throughout the meal. If you are a newcomer to Thai food, start off with something mild and then maybe work up to pig's intestine soup or chilli-flavoured serpents' heads! Also good to start with are curries (*kaeng phet*) – particularly those with a coconut-cream base, which are less piquant than Indian curries – and there is never any shortage of wonderful, fresh fish. There is no need to hold back on quantity or restrict yourself to one dish. Thais will usually order a selection and share them as a group.

When eating chillies, take a local tip and have plenty of steamed rice, which helps to soothe the stomach and will smother the fire. Nothing else is as effective, and cold drinks just make it worse.

Don't expect to find knives on Thai tables – a spoon is used instead. Sauces will be offered that you can use to

Street fare

On the whole, the best and certainly the cheapest meals will be found at food stalls which line the streets. Housewives buy their ingredients fresh and inexpensively at the market in the early morning and prepare their best dishes. There are usually no menus to choose from, as each stall offers a few specialities. Buying from food stalls poses no language difficulties, as you simply point at what you want. The food stalls may look rather dubious, but remember that unlike restaurants, everything is prepared before your very eyes. Westerners who have spent some time in Thailand have complete faith in these streetside stalls.

Try a variety of noodles at the many street stalls

season your dish instead of salt and pepper. One of them is *nam pla*, a salty caramel-coloured fish sauce with tiny chilli segments in it. *Nam phrik*, 'pepper water', is a much-prized concoction of pounded red chillies, shrimp paste, black pepper, garlic and onions mixed with tamarind, lemon juice, ginger and fish in an early state of fermentation.

Small bowls of roasted chillies are also served on the side for diners with a more robust constitution.

What to eat

Appetisers. *Paw pia tawt* is a Thai spring roll enclosing sweet-and-sour bean sprouts, pork and crabmeat. *Gai hor bai toey* consists of chicken chunks fried with sesame oil, soya sauce, oyster sauce, herbs and a drop of whisky, all in a leaf wrapper. *Krathong thong* are delicate mouth-size patty shells filled with a delicious combination of minced chicken, sweetcorn, carrots and soy sauce.

Som tam – a hot salad of papaya, chillies and shrimp or crab

Soup. *Tom yam* is a hot-sour soup, made with either pork, shrimp, chicken or fish, which should be accompanied by steamed rice to soak up the excess chilli heat. *Kaeng jeud* is a less pungent soup made from chicken, pork and shrimp cooked with Chinese-style vegetables, glass noodles and Thai herbs and spices. *Tom kha gai* is a midly spicy chicken soup with coconut milk and lemongrass. *Bah mee nam* is a rich broth of thin noodles, pork or chicken chunks, mixed with herbs, bean sprouts and subtle spices.

Rice and noodles. *Kao pad* is fried rice with bits of meat. *Mee grob* is crispy fried rice noodles with pork, egg, bean sprouts, shrimp, and a sweet-and-sour flavour. *Pad thai* is served many different ways, but is basically flat dried rice-flour noodles sautéed with garlic, onion, tamarind juice and a variety of spices, and served with vegetables.

Seafood. *Hor mok pla* is a fish curry with vegetables and coconut milk, served wrapped in banana leaves. *Pla preow*

wan is fried fish covered in a thick sweet-and-sour sauce. *Gung tod* – or crispy fried prawns – usually comes with a choice of sauces. *Pla samlee daet deow* is a whole deep-fried cotton-fish traditionally served with a tangy mango salad.

Chicken and meat. *Gaeng massaman* is a beef curry – less spicy than most – and has an overtone of peanuts. *Kao nah gai* is sliced chicken with spring onion, bamboo shoots and steamed rice. *Sa lad neua san* translates as roast beef salad

International fare

For a change of both taste and scenery, try one of the various Asian restaurants that serve a spectrum of different cuisines – many of them at bargain prices. By far the most common is Chinese. In Bangkok you can sample the most important regional schools of Chinese cooking – Sichuanese, Cantonese, Shanghainese and Pekingese – as well as the less familiar food of the Hakka, Chiu Chow and Hunan peoples.

Restaurants specialising in food from neighbouring Cambodia, Malaysia, Burma and Laos are not easy to find, but Japanese, Korean and Vietnamese food is well-represented.

The significant population of Thais of Indian descent or Muslim religion accounts for the availability of associated foods. In Bangkok there are several Indian cafés and restaurants to choose from, selling both northern and southern dishes.

In cities, especially Bangkok, and tourist-friendly areas such as Chiang Mai, Phuket, Pattaya and Samui, there will be a good choice of international food. Italian is the most popular non-Asian food by far, but there should also be options for French, German, Mexican and Californian, as well as pub grub.

The quality of international food is steadily improving, although prices are moving accordingly, and some restaurants are very high-end, including several spectacular rooftop outfits in Bangkok.

and contains vegetables, chillies, garlic and perhaps mint. *Kaeng ped gai naw mai* is red chicken curry with bamboo shoots, lime and basil leaves. *Kaeng ped* is roast duck curry, sometimes served with slices of fried aubergine.

Sweets. *Salim* is a refreshing sweet of sugared noodles with coconut milk and crushed ice. Ice cream, pronounced 'eye-cream', sometimes comes in original and natural flavours. A local variation of a sundae, for instance, is coconut ice cream sprinkled with peanuts and kernels of corn. *Khao tom mad* is sticky rice with coconut cream and bananas.

Fruit. *Somo* is a pomelo, a tropical cousin of the grapefruit, and is served divided into sections. *Sap-pa-rot*, or pineapple, is a familiar fruit but twice as tasty on its home ground. More exotic local fruits are rarely on restaurant menus, but can be discovered at markets and street stalls. Just point if you don't know the name. *Ngor* (rambutan) looks like

Hot and sour shrimp soup, tom yum goong

a hairy and overdeveloped strawberry; the fruit is inside. *Lamut*, a light-brown fruit that has to be peeled, is syrupy sweet, with a taste reminiscent of fresh figs. *Durian*, that green monster with spiky thorns, contains bits of custard-like fruit around egg-shaped piths. Its smell is often compared to that of a rubbish tip, although its creamy interior is deliciously sweet and luscious.

Mango, rice and coconut cream

Try local oranges, bananas, mangoes, papayas – almost every fruit imaginable, except apples and pears, which don't grow here and are expensive.

What to drink

Iced water is frequently served at the start of a meal. It's almost bound to be safe to drink in any decent restaurant, but if in doubt ask for a bottle of water and skip the ice (see page 122). Thais usually drink water or cold tea *(cha jin yen)* throughout their meal, along with beer or whisky with dinner.

Because of high import duty, wines are very expensive in Thailand, including the few locally produced labels. Even in a modest restaurant, an undistinguished wine could cost more than the whole dinner. Thailand also produces beer, such as Singha, Kloster and Chang – all stronger than you might expect.

Thai whisky, on the other hand, is weaker and cheaper than you'd think, and usually ordered by the small bottle in a 'set' with soda and ice. Mekhong is the best-known brand.

TO HELP YOU ORDER

Could we have a table? **Kor toh dai mai?**
I'd like a/an/some... **Chan yak dai ...**

beef **neua**	milk **nom**
beer **beer**	noodles **kwaytio**
bread **khanom-pang**	pork **moo**
chicken **kai**	rice **kao**
coffee **kafae**	salt **kleua**
curry **kaeng**	shrimp **kung**
egg **khai**	soup **soop**
fish **pla**	sugar **nam tan**
meat **neua**	tea **cha**
menu **maynu/raigarn**	water **nam**
arharn	wine **low wai**

Street food for sale in northern Thailand

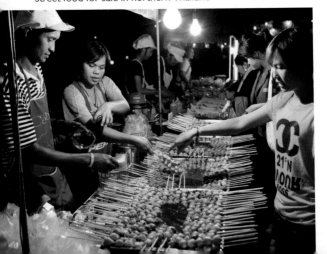

PLACES TO EAT

We have used the following symbols to give an idea of the price for a three-course meal for one, including wine, cover and service:

$$$$ over US$50   **$$** US$15–30
$$$ US$30–50   **$** less than US$15

BANGKOK

Le Beaulieu $$$ *50 Athénée Tower, 63 Wireless Road, tel: 0 2168 8220, www.le-beaulieu.com.* Open daily for lunch and dinner. With plates like slow-cooked mushroom ragout and New Zealand roast tenderloin in a sauce of veal jus, shallots, white port and pancetta, chef Hervé Frerard has forged one of the best reputations in town for French cuisine. Handily placed in Athénée Tower.

Biscotti $$$ *Four Seasons Hotel, 155 Ratchadamri Road, tel: 0 2126 8866 ext. 1229-30, www.fourseasons.com.* Open daily for lunch and dinner. One of the most popular Italian restaurants in Bangkok is casual but elegant with a contemporary flair and an open kitchen. There's a wood-fired oven for the inventive pizzas (such as the lobster tail pizza with forest mushrooms) and the fragrant *focaccia* bread with herbs. Risottos, pastas and a few meat dishes round out the menu.

Celadon $$$$ *The Sukhothai, 13/3 South Sathorn Road, tel: 0 2344 8888, www.sukhothai.com.* Open daily for lunch and dinner. Wonderfully located in the Zen-like Sukhothai hotel, overlooking a lotus pond. Here you can sample Royal Thai cuisine served by very knowledgeable staff who can help you combine dishes to create a most memorable meal. Banana blossom salad, spicy kingfish soup and sweet-and-sour tofu are just a few of the specialities. Desserts are outstanding.

China House $$$–$$$$ *The Mandarin Oriental hotel, 48 Oriental Avenue, tel: 0 2659 9000 ext. 739, www.mandarinoriental.*

com. Open Tue–Sun for lunch and dinner. The beautiful 1930s Shanghainese art deco interior features red lanterns, carved wood and ebony pillars. Miniature black-and-white photos and Chinese calligraphy cover the walls; a brass samovar steams in the central tearoom. It's a wonderful setting for top-quality dishes like hot-and-sour soup filled with fresh herbs and sweet lobster meat.

The Deck by the River $$–$$$ *Arun Residence, 36–38 Soi Pratoo Nok Yoong, tel: 0 2221 9158, www.arunresidence.com.* Open daily for lunch and dinner. Just two minutes' walk from Wat Pho, this cute place has outdoor seating, river views of Wat Arun and a bar, Amorosa, on the third floor. A mixed Thai and Euro fusion menu features plates such as carpaccio of tea-smoked duck. Book ahead (if you can) for a river table.

Grossi $$$ *InterContinental Bangkok, 973 Ploenchit Road, tel: 0 2656 0444, www.grossitrattoriabangkok.grossi.com.au.* Open daily for lunch and dinner. This Trattoria franchise of star Aussie chef Guy Grossi has an elegant deli ambiance. There's a floor of large black and white checks, marble counter displays of wines, bread and cold cuts, and a menu that eschews obvious Italian exports for dishes like burrata salad with anchovies and pressed beef cooked with chocolate and orange zest.

Harmonique $–$$ *22 Charoenkrung Soi 34, tel: 0 2237 8175.* Open Mon–Sat for lunch and dinner. Charming restaurant near the French Embassy occupying several old Chinese shophouses with leafy courtyards and filled with antiques. Because there's usually a large contingent of Western diners, the spices are subdued, but the food is generally good and it's handy for riverside hotels.

Long Table $$$ *Floor 25, The Column Residence, Sukhumvit Soi 16, tel: 0 2302 2557/9, www.longtablebangkok.com.* Open daily for lunch and dinner. Classy modern Thai restaurant designed with panache. Fantastic city views and a very long communal table are the focal points as you dine, while films on overhead monitors roll to a funky soundtrack. Yellow curry with crab and foie gras with dried shrimp and tamarind are both standouts.

Mango Tree $$ *37 Soi Tantawan, Surawongse Road, tel: 0 2236 2820, www.coca.com/mangotree.* Open daily for lunch and dinner. This lovely Thai restaurant is housed within a charming old house offering indoor/outdoor dining just steps from the busy Patpong neighbourhood. Specialities include fresh and spicy mango salad, chicken baked in pandanus leaf and a variety of green curries. There's Thai dancing on weekend evenings.

Nahm $$$$ *Metropolitan Hotel, 27 South Sathorn Road, tel: 0 2625 3388, www.metropolitan.bangkok.como.bz.* Open daily for lunch and dinner. Run by Australian chef David Thompson, this Thai restaurant is number 13 on the World's 50 Best Restaurants List (as of 2015). The traditional menu includes intriguing flavours that are becoming harder to find in modern Thai cooking, in regional dishes like jungle curry with snakehead fish and northern pork, prawn and tamarind relish.

New York Steakhouse $$$$ *JW Marriott Hotel, 4 Sukhumvit Soi 2, tel: 0 2656 7700, www.marriott.com.* Open daily for dinner. A pleasant and very contemporary restaurant serving the best steaks in the city. Aged to perfection, grain-fed Angus beef is flown in from the US along with excellent (and more affordable) Australian steaks. There's also a large selection of seafood including fresh lobster, swordfish and salmon.

Seafood Market and Restaurant $$$ *89 Sukhumvit Soi 24, Klongtoey, tel: 0 2261 2071, www.seafood.co.th.* In this seafood market-cum-restaurant you can select your dinner while it's still alive and have it cooked the way you like. Alternatively, those who don't dare to look their food in the eye may select dishes from the set menu. Stir-fried crab with curry powder and spicy soup with shrimps are recommended.

Sirocco $$$$ *63/F, Lebua at State Tower, 1055/111 Silom Road, tel: 0 2624 9555, www.lebua.com/sirocco.* Open daily for dinner. This spectacular 200 metre (656ft) -high rooftop restaurant has magnificent views of the river. Greco-Roman architecture and a jazz band add to the sense of occasion. While the food can be inconsistent, it is often excellent. In the same complex, there's the classy Distil Bar, the cocktail bar Ocean 52, the Italian eatery Mezzaluna, and the alfresco pan-Asian restaurant Breeze.

Sra Bua $$$$ *Siam Kempinski Hotel, 991/9 Rama I Road, tel: 0 2162 9000, www.kempinskibangkok.com.* Open daily for lunch and dinner. This branch of Copenhagen's Michelin-starred Kiin Kiin has a playful approach to Thai food. Dishes are artfully presented – a green curry mousse in a flower pot, soups served as tiny jellies and red curry ice-cream. Centrally located behind Siam Paragon shopping mall.

Tables Grill $$$$ *Grand Hyatt Erawan Hotel, 494 Ratchadamri Road, tel: 0 2254 1234, www.bangkok.grand.hyatt.com.* Open daily for lunch and dinner. Oxidised mirrors and waiters in white aprons aid the smart Parisian interior in this restaurant designed by Tony Chi. Billed as classic European, it's full of old stalwarts like Sunday roast, lobster bisque and champagne risotto. Chefs cook some dishes in the open at copper-topped tables.

CHIANG MAI

The Gallery $$ *25–29 Charoenrat Road, tel: 0 5324 8601, www. thegallery-restaurant.com.* Open daily from noon–midnight. This lovely restaurant is located on the banks of the River Ping in an old teakwood house that doubles as an art gallery. There's a wide variety of northern Thai dishes as well as a good selection of vegetarian specialities, plus a small wine list.

Huen Phen $ *112 Rachamankha, tel: 0 5381 4548.* Open daily for lunch and dinner. This old wooden house located just inside the old city walls is decorated with local antiques and is reputed to serve some of the best northern Thai dishes in Chiang Mai. Good picks are *laap khua* (spicy minced-pork salad) and *kaeng hang-leh* (savoury, Burmese-influenced curry).

PHUKET

Baan Rim Pa $$$$ *223 Prabaramee Road, Patong, tel: 0 7634*

0789, www.baanrimpa.com. Open daily for lunch and dinner. Exquisitely prepared Thai food from a restaurant on a cliff overlooking the ocean. It includes such specialities as steamed fish in pickled-plum sauce and hot-and-sour soup with fish and vegetables. Also has a good selection of vegetarian dishes.

Boathouse Wine & Grill $$$ *182 Koktanode Road, Kata Beach, tel: 0 7633 0015*, www.boathousephuket.com. Open daily 11am–11pm. Offering fine views of the Andaman Sea, this beach-front restaurant offers refined Thai and European dining as well as seafood specialties. There is also a large wine selection, and indoor and outdoor seating is available.

Tamarind Spa Restaurant $$ *Banyan Tree Phuket, 33, 33/27 Moo 4, Srisoonthorn Road, Cherngtalay, Amphur Talang, tel: 0 7637 2400*, www.banyantree.com. Open daily for lunch and dinner. This cool, airy and shaded restaurant is located alongside the serene and Zen-like lap pool at a luxurious resort hotel. The unusual (but very affordable) menu features low-calorie specialities such as soba-noodle salad with fresh greens, vegetable juice cocktails and delicious sandwiches. Only the freshest market ingredients are used, along with local herbs and spices, to add a subtle fusion of Thai flavours to every dish.

KO SAMUI

The Beach Club $$$ *BuriRasa Village Resort & Spa, 11/2 Moo 2 Chaweng Beach, tel: 0 7723 0222*, www.burirasa.com. Open daily for lunch and dinner. This smart, wooden beachside restaurant with some tables on the sands plates modern Californian/Pacific Rim dishes. Specialities include scallops duck with black rice and soba noodles with seared ahi tuna. Desserts like chocolate air cake with tonka bean ice cream are exquisite.

The Boudoir $$$ *Soi 1 Mae Nam, tel: 8 5783 1031*. Owned by an expatriate couple from France, this small cosy restaurant with flamboyant decor serves enjoyable French fare. It is a romantic setting for alfresco dining. Slightly off the beaten track, but well worth a visit.

Poppies Restaurant $$$ *Poppies Samui resort, Chaweng Beach, tel: 0 7742 2419*, www.poppiessamui.com. Open daily for lunch and dinner. One of the most romantic restaurants on the island is right on the beach and serves Thai cuisine infused with a Western twist, such as the popular prawn cakes with plum sauce and charcoal-roasted duck. There's also an excellent selection of fusion dishes such as the chicken filled with crabmeat and baked in a seafood sauce.

CHIANG RAI

Salung Kham $$ *384/3 Paholyothin Road, tel: 0 5371 7192*, www.salungkham.com. Open daily for lunch and dinner. The Northern Thai menu includes Chiang Rai sausage, curries, and steamed herbal chicken with bamboo shoots. The indoor section is decorated with Thai handicrafts and there is also a pleasant garden.

MAE HONG SON

Fern Restaurant $ *87 Khunlumpraphat Road, tel: 0 5361 1374*. This rustic restaurant near Jong Kum Lake is one of the town's best. The house speciality is tasty and crunchy fern shoots, served either stir-fried or as a spicy warm salad. The typically spicy dishes are cooked with a deft touch and are not too overpowering.

HUA HIN

Brasserie de Paris $$$ *3 Naresdamri Road, tel: 0 3253 0637*, www.brasseriedeparis.net. Open daily for lunch and dinner. Sit upstairs at this wooden pier restaurant for views of fishing boats bobbing on the waves. It has delicious, freshly caught seafood served French-style, such as rock lobster *au beurre blanc*.

Chao Lay $$–$$$ *15 Naresdamri Road, tel: 0 3251 3436*. Open daily for lunch and dinner. One of the most popular of several Thai restaurants on stilts over the sea. The menu features all kinds of seafood, grilled, deep-fried and steamed, either freshly caught or live from tanks downstairs.

A–Z TRAVEL TIPS

A Summary of Practical Information

A

ACCOMMODATION

Thailand's accommodation rates vary widely in each category, so shop around for bargains. In high season, from November to March, it is best to book well ahead. Prices are high and many hotels have a compulsory gala dinner at Christmas and New Year. In low season discounts in excess of 50 percent are common, although hotels in less visited places may close for part of the time.

Top-end hotels are generally excellent and even mid-range and budget lodgings will often have a pool. The term 'resort' in Thailand may merely translate as a countryside or beachside location, and may not imply all the features you'd expect. High-end and mid-range places charge 10 percent service and seven percent VAT.

Serviced apartments, available in major destinations, can save money while having many facilities you'd find in a hotel. There is a serviced apartment list by area at www.sabaai.com. New design-conscious properties have widened the choice of accommodation, and many places have villas in both beach and jungle settings. Guesthouses often provide clean and decent rooms, while the Deep South islands have beach huts with perhaps only a fan and cold shower, but the natural scenery amply compensates. Rangers huts in national parks can also be very cheap.

Youth hostels are found in Bangkok and Chiang Mai, and to a lesser extent in Ayutthaya, Kanchanaburi and Phuket. The International Youth Hostel Federation has a Thailand page (www.tyha.org) with hostel listings. Thailand is also expanding its range in home stays and eco tourism, where visitors interact more with the local community. These are largely village initiatives, such as Ban Mae Kampong (tel: 0 5322 952; www.mae-kampong.com) in Chiang Mai and Ayutthaya's Ban Rang Jorakae (tel: 0 3530 5441).

Do you have a (double) room? **Mee hong (kuu) mai?**

AIRPORTS

Air service to Bangkok is excellent with non-stop flights arriving daily from London, Sydney, the US, many European, and most Asian cities. **Suvarnabhumi Airport** (pronounced 'su-wan-na-poom'; BKK; call centre tel: 0 2132 1888; www.suvarnabhumiairport.com) is approximately 30km (19 miles) east of the city. It handles all international flights to Bangkok as well as many domestic connections.

Air-conditioned taxis are available from the counter outside the arrival hall. Tell the desk clerk your destination and this will be written in Thai on a slip and handed to the driver. Make sure the driver turns on the meter. There will be an airport surcharge of B50 payable to the driver on arrival. If you have agreed to use the expressway, there will be extra toll fees (B70). The trip from the airport to Bangkok's hotels takes about 40 minutes. Expect to pay B250–350 to reach the city centre.

The Suvarnabhumi Airport Rail Link (SARL) opened in 2010. There are three services: the City Line, calling at eight stations en route to Phaya Thai; and the Express Line direct to Bangkok City Air Terminal, at Makkasan, where passengers can check in and drop luggage, and another Express Line to Phaya Thai. Tickets are B15–45 (City Line) and B150 (Express Line; round trip) with journey times of 30 minutes, 15 and 17 minutes respectively. The trains run from 6am until midnight.

BMTA Buses run from 5am until 10pm–2pm along five routes: to Happy Land, Samuthprakarn, Rangsit (2 lines), Samae Dam Garage. Tickets are B32–34. The transfer bus service to Don Muaeng Airport (old Bangkok International Airport; http://donmueangairportthai.com) operates between 5am and midnight and is free of charge.

Chiang Mai International Airport (CNX; tel: 0 5327 0222; http://chiangmaiairportthai.com) is 6km (4 miles) west of the city. To get to the city centre, order a taxi (B120–150, rides are not metered in Chiang Mai) or hail a 'red car' (*rot daeng* or *song thae*; usually B20), which is a van like vehicle with two parallel bench seats inside.

Phuket International Airport (HKT; tel: 0 7632 7230; http://phuket airportthai.com) is 28km (18 miles) north of Phuket Town. Metered

red-and-yellow taxis take 30 minutes (around B400) to Phuket Town or beaches. Buses run from 9am until 8pm to Phuket Town only. Tickets are B100 and the journey takes around one hour (www.airportbus phuket.com). **Hat Yai International Airport** (HDY; tel: 0 7425 1007 12; http://hatyaiairportthai.com) is a major airport in southern Thailand. **Ko Samui Airport** (USM; tel: 0 7742 5012; www.samuiairporton line.com), privately owned, is 5km (3 miles) north of Chaweng Beach.

B

BICYCLE AND MOPED HIRE

Although cycling is difficult in Bangkok traffic, bikes can be rented at several hotels and guesthouses. In Ayutthaya, Pattaya, Ko Samui, Phuket and Chiang Mai, bikes and mopeds are more readily available at roadside outlets. Spice Roads (tel: 0 2381 7490; www.spiceroads. com) has bicycles for hire.

BUDGETING FOR YOUR TRIP

Bangkok is inexpensive when compared to most major cities. There are approximately 47 *baht* to 1 pound, 30 *baht* to the US dollar.
Transport. Taxi: 40–200 *baht*.
Metro, Skytrain 15–42 *baht* per trip.
Domestic one-way flight example: Bangkok to Phuket 2,200 *baht*.
Domestic rail ticket example: Bangkok to Surat Thani 519 *baht* (first class), 107 *baht* (third class).
Domestic bus ticket example: Bangkok to Chiang Mai 510 *baht*.
A short *tuk-tuk* fare: 30–50 *baht*.
Meals. You can save lots of money by eating street food, and in many cases it is tastier, too. A meal will cost between 30–100 *baht*, half the price of a budget diner. Main courses in moderate international restaurants are 300–750 *baht*, and in expensive restaurants 900–2,500 *baht*. The cheapest bottle of wine in a restaurant is around 800 *baht*, while beer in a pub is 50–200 *baht*.

Other money saving tips are to use multi-trip passes on the Bangkok Skytrain and Metro, and check bars and restaurant websites for cheap deals, even in hotels, as entertainment competition is fierce.

C

CAMPING

Several national parks offer camping facilities, with prices starting around B60 for two people, plus an extra B90 for a tent. Don't camp outside campgrounds as robberies are not uncommon. Find a list of national parks at www.dnp.go.th, where you can also book accommodation, or contact the local TAT office (see page 129).

CAR HIRE (see also Driving)

Although driving can be stressful in Thailand many roads are excellent, making car hire a realistic idea, particularly in the countryside.

Several international hire companies operate in Thailand, including **Avis** (2/12-13 Wireless Road, Bangkok, tel: 0 2251 1131, www.avis thailand.com), **Budget** (201/2 Mahidol Road, Chiang Mai, tel: 0 5320 2871, www.budget.co.th) and **Hertz** (72/8-9 North Sathorn Road, Bangkok, tel: 0 2266 4666, www.hertzthailand.com), with rates starting around B950 a day. Local firms, such as **Phuket Car Rent** (23/3 Moo 1 Sakoo, Thalang, Phuket, tel: 0 7620 5190, www.phuketcarrent.com) and **Sathorn Car Rent** (6/8-9 Sathorn Nua Rd, Silom Bangrak, Bangkok, tel: 0 2633 8888, www.sathorncarrent.com) start from B800 a day, but check insurance is included (opt for the full package, including Collision Damage Waiver).

It is possible to hire a vehicle with driver, from an extra B300–500 per day, plus a surcharge for overnight stays.

CLIMATE

Thailand has three seasons: hot from March to May, rainy from June to October, and cool from November to February. For tourists from more temperate regions, it is just plain hot, amplified by humidity levels above 70 percent. The countryside is generally milder, with Chiang Mai having cool season temperatures of 13–28°C (55–82°F). The height of the rainy season is September, with over 300mm (11.8 inches) of rainfall in Bangkok and over 400mm in the south. The Gulf, around Ko Samui, receives only light rain from June to October and has a second high season in June and July.

	J	F	M	A	M	J	J	A	S	O	N	D
av. max. (°F)	89	91	93	95	93	91	90	90	89	88	87	87
av. max. (°C)	32	33	34	35	34	33	32	32	32	31	31	31
av. min. (°F)	68	72	75	77	77	76	76	76	76	75	72	68
av. min. (°C)	20	22	24	25	25	24	24	24	24	24	22	20
rainy days	2	2	4	5	14	16	19	21	23	17	7	1

CLOTHING

Light and loose clothes are best for Thailand, preferably of natural fibres, which breathe better. A hat will protect from the sun, and it's best to carry a light mac or umbrella during the rainy season. Convenience stores sell them if you get caught out.

Open-toed sandals, shorts and bare shoulders are not allowed in temples, but temples in tourist areas often hire out appropriate attire for a small fee. A shirt and tie are expected for business appointments, but in most restaurants even jeans and a T-shirt will be OK. Some people do go topless on beaches, but it is illegal.

CRIME AND SAFETY (See also Emergencies)

Thailand is generally very safe, although a few precautions are wise. Beware of pickpockets in crowded marketplaces, carry bags away from the roadside to thwart motorbike bag-snatchers, and don't be flash with money, particularly around red-light areas. It is advisable to avoid the southern provinces of Narathiwat, Yala, Pattani and Songkhla, where there is a high risk of Muslim separatist violence. You should also better refrain from trips to Preah Vihear and Ta Krabey temples, which are subject to the Cambodian–Thai border dispute.

Thais tend to be non-confrontational, so casual harassment and sexual crimes against women are uncommon. That said, like any-where, it isn't a great idea to walk alone on quiet streets or beaches late at night. Thailand has tough drug laws; indulge at your peril. In times of trouble it is best to contact the Tourist Police hotline: 1155.

D

DISABLED TRAVELLERS

Thailand is a major challenge for disabled travellers, and a compan-ion is highly advisable. Pavements are often uneven and crowded with obstructions, and there are few wheelchair ramps in buildings. There are no facilities to speak of in any of the transport networks. Wheelchair Tours to Thailand (tel: 0 2720 5395; www.wheelchair tours.com) specialises in package tours for the disabled.

DRIVING

Road conditions. Driving in Thailand is on the left; overtake and give way to the right. Highway tolls apply to some expressway sec-tions, especially in Bangkok. Roads are generally in good condition but main routes are very busy. There is only a rudimentary driving test, however, so drivers largely learn by intuition. Road courtesy is low, with right-of-way determined by size. Tailgating and dangerous overtaking are also common. That said, once you are acclimatised, driving in Thailand is not too uncomfortable.

Rules and regulations. Visitors need an International Driver's Li-cence. The official speed limit is 50kph (30mph) in towns, 80kph (50mph) on main roads and 120kph (70mph) on motorways. Seat belts are compulsory. Drink driving is against the law, with an alco-hol limit of 50mg per 100 millilitres. The law requires that if you have an accident, you don't move the vehicle to the side of the road, but leave everything as it is, so police can make an assessment.

Fuel. Readily available in both regular and super.

Parking. If stuck for somewhere to park on the street, try a temple, as they often have public parking spaces for a small fee.

If you need help. Telephone the agency from which you rented the car to come and rescue you. In an emergency dial the Tourist Police hotline: 1155 or the Highway Police Patrol Centre, tel: 1193.

Road signs. Most road signs are in English.

accident **u-bat-fi-het**
collision **rot chon**
flat tyre **yang baen**
Help! **chuey duey!**
Police! **tam ruat**!

E

ELECTRICITY

The standard current in Thailand is 220-volt, 50-cycle AC. Most hotel rooms have an electrical outlet for shavers; some have 110-volt sockets, too. Plugs are two-pin and you'll need adaptors (and transformers depending on where you're coming from).

EMBASSIES AND CONSULATES

Australia: 37 South Sathorn Road, Bangkok, tel: 0 2344 6300, www. thailand.embassy.gov.au.

Canada: 990 Rama IV Road, Abdulrahim Place, 15th Floor, Bangkok, tel: 0 2646 4300, www.canadainternational.gc.ca.

Ireland Honorary Consul: tel: 02 6326720, www.irelandinthailand. com.

New Zealand: M Thai Tower, 14th Floor, All Seasons Place, 87

Wireless Road, Bangkok, tel: 0 2254 2530, www.nzembassy.com.
South Africa: M Thai Tower, 12th Floor, All Seasons Place, 87 Wireless Road, Bangkok, tel: 0 2659 2900; www.dirco.gov.za/bangkok.
UK: 14 Wireless Road, Bangkok, tel: 0 2305 8333, www.ukinthailand.
fco.gov.uk.
US: 95 Wireless Road, Bangkok, tel: 0 2205 4000, http://bangkok.
usembassy.gov.

EMERGENCIES

In case of an emergency dial **191**. For less dire emergencies, contact the Tourist Police on **1155**.

G

GAY AND LESBIAN TRAVELLERS

Thai people's general tolerance towards others extends to sexual orientation and gay lifestyles, particularly in Bangkok, are highly visible and very relaxed. There are many gay clubs and bars, and a lively party scene amid the terrace drinkers of Silom Soi 4. Chiang Mai and Phuket also have several gay-friendly venues. *Katoeys* (ladyboys) are similarly high profile. The lesbian scene is more discreet, but there are a few women-only places in Bangkok. There are on-off Gay Pride Festivals in Bangkok, Phuket and Pattaya. Useful resources are www.
utopia-asia.com; www.bangkoklesbian.com and the specialist gay travel company Purple Dragon (www.purpledrag.com).

GETTING THERE

Air travel. Suvarnabhumi Airport (see Airports) is the main gateway to Thailand. From the UK, the main airlines flying direct are British Airways (www.britishairways.com) and Thai Airways International (THAI) (www.thaiairways.com), all from London Heathrow, with a flight time of around 11 hours.

From Australia, Qantas flies from Sydney (9hrs) and Thai Airways flies from Brisbane (9hrs), Melbourne (9hrs), Perth (7hrs) and Sydney (9hrs).

From the US, Thai Airways flies direct from Los Angeles (17hrs). The best deals for all flights are online at sites such as FareCompare (www.farecompare.com) or Travel Supermarket.Com (www.travel supermarket.com).

International airports. Phuket, Chiang Mai and Samui handle international flights from Asian cities like Hong Kong and Singapore.

Rail travel. Comfortable trains run from Singapore to Bangkok, including the luxury service run by the Venice-Simplon Orient Express, known as the Eastern and Oriental Express.

H

HEALTH AND MEDICAL CARE

No vaccinations are required to enter Thailand. Malaria and dengue persist in rural areas but less so in Bangkok. When in the countryside, especially in the monsoon season, apply mosquito repellent on exposed skin at all times – dengue mosquitoes are most active in the day.

Never drink the tap water anywhere in the country. Bottled water is readily available everywhere. Responsible restaurants serve bottled water and pure ice, but be cautious about the ice in drinks at roadside stands.

Many Westerners suffer some kind of intestinal discomfort from the spicy food, the excessive heat and the unusual ingredients. Spare your digestive system by experimenting gradually until you're more accustomed to the Thai cuisine. Avoiding fresh vegetables and unpeeled fruit is a good idea except at the top hotels and restaurants, and avoid uncooked foods at market stalls.

Ensure you buy health insurance before travelling. Most major hospitals in Thailand accept credit cards and are of a high standard in Bangkok and other cities, and there's always a pharmacy open 24 hours. Prices for medical services are significantly below equivalent charges in Europe and the US. Pharmacies nationwide are well-equipped and can dispense over the counter many medications that require prescriptions in Western countries.

> a bottle of drinking water **nam yen neung khuad**
> I need a doctor **pom/chan tong karn maw**
> I need a dentist **pom/chan tong karn maw fan**

L

LANGUAGE

Although English is widely used in hotels and shops and is the best-known Western language in Thailand, try to use some simple phrases in Thai. The Thai language spoken in Bangkok is understood everywhere in the country, though there are many dialects and sub-dialects. Like Chinese, Thai uses intonation to distinguish between otherwise identical words, which makes it a difficult language for foreigners. Each syllable can have up to five different meanings depending on how it is pronounced; there are 44 consonants plus dozens of vowels, compounds and tone marks. If all this doesn't discourage you, consider Rachasap, a special language used only when speaking to or about Thai royalty!

Listen to Thai people to learn how to intone useful words. You will find a brief list of useful expressions below.

Numbers

one **neung**	seven **jet**
two **sorng**	eight **(b)paet**
three **sarm**	nine **gao**
four **see**	ten **sip**
five **har**	eleven **sip-eht**
six **hok**	twelve **sip-sorng**

thirteen **sip-sarm**	thirty **sarm-sip**
fourteen **sip-see**	forty **see-sip**
fifteen **sip-har**	fifty **har-sip**
sixteen **sip-hok**	sixty **hok-sip**
seventeen **sip-jet**	seventy **jet-sip**
eighteen **sip-(b)paet**	eighty **(b)paet-sip**
nineteen **sip-gao**	ninety **gao-sip**
twenty **yee-sip**	one hundred **roy**

Days of the week

Monday **wan jan**	Friday **wan suk**
Tuesday **wan ang karn**	Saturday **wan sow**
Wednesday **wan put**	Sunday **wan ar tit**
Thursday **wan pa ru hat**	

thank you **korp khun kap (if you are a man) ka (if you are a woman)**

hello/goodbye **sawatdee kap (if you are a man) ka (if you are a woman)**

today **wan nee**

tomorrow **prung nee**

good/bad **dee/lehw**

big/small **yai/lek**

cheap/expensive **took/phaeng**

hot/cold **rorn/yen**

quick/slow **rehw/char**

When does ... open/close? **... pert/pit meua rai?**

What's the fare to ...? **(b)pai ... kit thao rai?**

stop here **jop teenee**

turn right **lieo khwa**

turn left **lieo sai**

Could you speak more slowly? **Poot char long dai mai?**

I don't understand **mai kao chai**

I'm sorry/excuse me **kor thort**

M

MAPS

The Tourism Authority of Thailand (see page 129) issues free bus and tourist maps showing the principal attractions of Bangkok. These aren't always adequate, though, and it is better to buy one of the commercially produced maps of Bangkok and Thailand that are sold at hotels and bookshops. Interesting specialised maps of the waterways and markets of Bangkok are also available. For quirkiness, check out Groovy Maps and Nancy Chandler's maps.

MEDIA

The *Bangkok Post* and *The Nation* are Thailand's leading English-language newspapers. They are available at most hotels and airports and are updated daily online at www.bangkokpost.com and www.nationmultimedia.com. Useful listings magazines include BK (www.bk.asia-city.com) for Bangkok, Citylife (www.chiangmainews.com) in Chiang Mai, and Pattaya Mail (www.pattayamail.com).

There are six terrestrial Bangkok TV channels, and many programmes are foreign shows, which are dubbed into Thai. There is also a cable television network with international channels, including BBC News, HBO, ESPN, and MTV Thailand, that is available in most leading hotels. Radio stations include Fat Radio (104.5 FM) featuring Thai indie music, Eazy FM (105.5FM), with middle-of-the road music, and Virgin HITZ/FMX (95.5 FM) playing contemporary dance and pop.

MONEY

Currency. The unit of currency in Thailand is the baht (abbreviated THB, Bt or B), divided into 100 satang. Banknotes come in denominations of 20, 50, 100, 500 and 1,000 baht. Coins are 25 and 50 *satang*, and 1, 2, 5 and 10 *baht*.

Banks and exchange facilities. Normally the exchange rate at banks is the most favourable. After the banks are closed you can change money at your hotel, at exchange booths or at shops displaying a sign in English saying 'money changer'.

Banks and money-changers in tourist towns will accept virtually any major currency.

Credit cards. Major hotels, restaurants and shops are accustomed to the well-known international charge cards. Small eateries and small shops tend to accept cash only.

ATMs. Facilities for using your debit or credit card to withdraw money automatically are widely available in Thailand, especially in Bangkok and at the major airports.

O

OPENING HOURS

Business hours are 8.30am–noon and 1–4.30pm, Monday–Friday for government offices. Banks are open 8.30am–3.30pm. Department stores are usually open 10am–10pm seven days a week. Hours are extended just before Christmas, New Year and Chinese New Year. In seaside tourist areas, many shops are open from early in the morning until 11pm or even midnight during the high season. Note that many state-run museums are closed on Monday and Tuesday.

P

POLICE

A special force of Thai Tourist Police operates in crucial areas of Bangkok and throughout the country, such as near tourist attractions and major hotels. The officers, all of whom speak passable English, stand ready to protect or advise foreigners. They wear the beige military-style uniform of ordinary Thai police, but with 'Tourist Police' shoulder patches. Dial 1155 from any phone in the country to reach the Tourist Police. The Royal Thai Police Headquarters is at Rama 1 Road, Pathumwan Bangkok, tel: 0 2253 2244.

POST OFFICES

Bangkok's main post office is open 8am–8pm Monday–Friday, and 8am–1pm Saturday–Sunday. Branch offices, found at airports and throughout the country, are usually open Mon–Fri 8am–4.30pm and Sat 9am–noon. You can send letters and postcards airmail, which should arrive within five days to a week in Europe or North America. Many newspaper shops sell stamps and there are red post boxes on the streets.

PUBLIC HOLIDAYS

Since many Thai holidays and festivals are fixed to the lunar calendar, the dates vary from year to year. Banks are closed on these days, but daily life is not necessarily disrupted. The only notable exception is Chinese New Year, a time when most businesses are closed.

1 January **New Year's Day**
6 April **Chakri Day, honouring Rama I**
13–15 April **Songkran (Water Festival)**
1 May **Labour Day**
5 May **Coronation Day**
12 August **HM the Queen's Birthday**
23 October **Chulalongkorn Day, honouring Rama V**
5 December **HM the King's Birthday and National Day**
10 December **Constitution Day**
31 December **New Year's Eve**

Variable dates
Chinese New Year (1st month of the lunar calendar, usually Jan/Feb).
Maka Puja (full moon in February). Commemoration of meeting at which the Buddha preached the doctrines of Buddhism.
Visakha Puja (full moon in May). Celebrates the birth, enlightenment and death of the Buddha. Most holy Buddhist ceremonial day.
Asanha Puja (full moon in July). Celebrates Buddha's first sermon.

T

TELEPHONES

Thailand's country code is 66. To make an overseas phone call from Thailand first dial 001 followed by the country code (without the preceding 0) and area code. If you need international call assistance, dial 100. To avoid hotel surcharges on phone calls, call from one of the public telephones located on streets and in post offices. Rates (usually per minute with a 3-minute minimum) are posted in English. Prepaid international phone cards can also be used. These can be bought at post offices, 7 Eleven stores, shops displaying the ThaiCard sign and the office of the Communications Authority of Thailand (tel: 1322, www.cattelecom.com). For local directory assistance, dial 1133.

Mobile phones. Users of mobiles with international roaming facility can hook up automatically to the local Thai network. Check with your service provider if you are unsure. As roaming rates are bound to be high, an alternative is to buy a local SIM card with a stored value from a mobile phone shop. Local mobile network operators include: AIS (www.ais.co.th), DTAC (www.dtac.co.th) and True (http://www3.truecorp.co.th).

TIME ZONE

Thailand time is GMT plus 7 hours throughout the year. When it's noon in Bangkok in winter, it's 9pm the day before in Los Angeles, midnight in New York, 5am in London and 4pm in Sydney.

TIPPING

Tipping is not generally a custom in Thailand, although it is more prevalent in Bangkok, Phuket and Pattaya. Restaurants (not small Thai places) and hotels will add a service charge of 10 percent to your bill. People leave loose change left over from their bill both in cafés and taxis. Otherwise, tip massage therapists and hairdressers 10 percent and maids, porters and parking attendants B20.

TOILETS

Try to find a hotel or restaurant. In luxury establishments the toilets are spotless. Away from the main centres, you will encounter hole-in-the-floor toilets. In places without running water, you will always find a huge jar of water nearby. Scoop water out for flushing and washing. Some public toilets are free.

Where are the toilets? **Hong nam yu tee nai?**

TOURIST INFORMATION

The **Tourism Authority of Thailand (TAT)** runs information stands in the arrivals hall of Suvarnabhumi, Chiang Mai and Phuket airports.

You can also obtain leaflets, maps and advice at the organisation's head office: 1600 New Phetburi Road, Makkasan, Ratchathewi, Bangkok 10400; daily 8.30am–4.30pm, tel: 0 2250 5500 or 1672, www.tourismthailand.org. Other Bangkok branches are located in the building of the Ministry of Tourism and Sports (4 Ratchadamnoen Nok Road, Wat Somanat, Pom Prap Sattru Phai; daily 8.30am –4.30pm), Suvarnabhumi Airport Gate 3 and Gate 10 (both open 24 hours).

Branch offices of TAT are also located in Chiang Mai, Kanchanaburi, Nakhon Ratchasima (Korat), Pattaya, Ko Samui and Phuket. In Chiang Mai the address is: 105/1 Chiang Mai-Lamphun Road, tel: 0 5324 8604, and in Phuket, 191 Thalang Road, Phuket Town; tel: 0 7621 1036.

Overseas representatives of TAT can be found in the following countries:
Australia: Level 20, 56 Pitt Street, Sydney 2000, tel: +61-2-9247 7549, www.thailand.net.au.
UK: 1st Floor, 17-19 Cockspur Street, Trafalgar Square, London SW1Y 5BL; tel: +44-207-925 2511, www.tourismthailand.co.uk.
US: 611 North Larchmont Boulevard, Los Angeles, CA 90004, tel: 1-323-461 9814; 61 Broadway, Suite 2810, New York, NY 10006, tel: 1-212-432 0433.

TRANSPORT

Domestic Flights. The main domestic airline is Thai Airways (tel: 0 2356 1111, 0 2288 7000, www.thaiairways.com), followed by Bangkok Airways (tel: 0 2270 6699 or 1771, www.bangkokair.com). Budget airlines are Nok Air (tel: 1318 or 0 2900 9955, www.nokair.com), Air Asia (tel: 0 2515 9999, www.airasia.com) and Orient Thai (tel: 0 2229 4260 or 1126, http://flyorientthai.com).

Ferries. The main ferries are from the mainland to the Gulf islands of Ko Samui, Ko Phangan and Ko Chang. Seatran Ferry (tel: 0 7725 1555, 0 2240 2582, www.seatranferry.com) from Donsak to Ko Samui runs 14 boats a day, 6am–7pm, with tickets at B130 for passengers, and B420 for a car with a driver. Koh Chang Ferry (tel: 0 3952 8288) runs from Laem Ngop to Ko Chang 6.30am–5pm. Passenger return tickets are B120, cars B150.

Trains. Thailand's state railway (tel: 0 2222 0175, hotline: 1690, www.railway.co.th) is an efficient means of seeing the country, although for many routes, buses are quicker. Travel agents, hotel desks and the information office at the main (Hualamphong) railway station can advise you on timetables and fares. Bangkok's main stations are: Hualamphong on Rama IV Road, for the north, east and northeast and for express trains to the south, and Thonburi on Bangkok Noi on Rod Fai Road, for the west and slower trains to the south.

Popular routes are Bangkok to Chiang Mai (8.30am–10pm, first class fare B593) and Bangkok to Ayutthaya (4.20am–10.25pm, B66).

Intercity coaches. Government buses are operated by the Transport Company Ltd (tel: 1490, www.transport.co.th). They are known locally as Bor Kor Sor (BKS), and have terminals at every town. Buy tickets (VIP, 1st and 2nd classes) at any BKS station or online from www.thaiticketmajor.com.

Popular routes include Bangkok to Phuket (14 hours) and Bangkok to Chiang Mai (11 hours).

Skytrain (BTS). The Bangkok Transit System (Tourist Information Centre: tel: 0 2617 7341, hotline: 0 2617 6000, www.bts.co.th) is an elevated train service, better known as Skytrain. Trains operate from 6am–midnight. Single-trip fares vary according to distance, starting at B15 and rising to B42. Self-service ticket machines are found at all station concourses. Tourists may find it useful to buy the unlimited ride 1-Day Pass (B130) or the 30-Day Adult Pass (which comes in four types: B405 for 15 rides, B625 for 25, B920 for 40 and B1,100 for 50). The 30-day pass should be added to a Rabbit Card, which you will need to purchase (B50, from 2016 B150). All available at station counters.

Metro (MRT or subway). Bangkok's metro line (Customer Relations: tel: 0 2624 5200, www.bangkokmetro.co.th) operates from 6am to midnight. Fares start at B16, increasing B2–3 every station, with a maximum fare of B42. You can buy passes with unlimited rides: the 1-Day Pass (B120), 3-Day Pass (B230), 30-Day Pass (B1,400) and the stored-value Adult Card (B230, includes a B50 deposit).

Taxis. Taxis in Bangkok are metered, air-conditioned and inexpensive. The flag fall is B35 for the first km, then B5.5–8 per kilometre, depending on distance travelled. If stuck in traffic, a small per-minute (usually B2) surcharge kicks in. It's best to hail them on the streets, as those parked outside hotels often hustle for a no-meter fare. Fares, however, are negotiated for longer distances outside Bangkok: for instance, to Pattaya (B1,500), Koh Samet (B2,500) or Hua Hin (3,000). The following taxi companies will take bookings for a B20 surcharge: Siam Taxi (hotline: 1661), Nakhornthai Transportation (tel: 0 2878 9000).

Tuk-Tuks. Tuk-tuks are brightly coloured three-wheeled taxis. Negotiate the fare before you set off. In Bangkok, expect to pay B30–50 for short journeys of around 10 minutes or less, and B50–200 for longer journeys. Tuk-tuks, along with *songthaew* are the best and sometimes only way of getting around upcountry, as many towns have no bus service.

Songthaew. *Songthaew* are pick-up trucks with two benches in the back and operate like buses, usually with a loose route, but occasionally able to make detours. Hail one on the street and state your destination. Fares start around B8–12. Bargain for a price before you get in.

Motorcycle taxis. Motorcycle taxi stands are noticeable by their drivers – a gathering of men in fluorescent, numbered vests found at the mouth of many sois. Short journeys, such as the length of a street, will cost B10–30. Longer rides (B80–200 should get you a half-hour trip) are more expensive during rush hour (8–10am and 4–6pm).

Buses. In Bangkok buses come in air conditioned or non-air conditioned varieties. Municipal and private operators all come under the charge of the Bangkok Mass Transit Authority (tel: 1348 or 0 2246 0339, www.bmta.co.th). Chiang Mai also has several bus routes, but most towns rely on tuk-tuks and *songthaew*.

Boats. Bangkok's most common waterborne transport is the Chao Phraya Express Boat Company (tel: 0 2445 8888, www.chaophraya expressboat.com), which runs services between Nonthaburi pier in the north to Ratburana in the south. Boats run every 10–20 minutes 6am–8pm, and stop at different piers according to the coloured flag on top of the boat. Yellow and green flags are fastest, but stop at only 12 piers, while orange flags are slowest but stop at every pier. Sat and Sun have only orange-flagged boats. There is also no flag route from Nonthaburi to Wat Rajsinkorn. Tickets cost B10–32 and are purchased from the conductor on board or at some pier counters. The company also offers sightseeing boat tours. The Chao Phraya Tourist Boat operates daily 9.30am–4.30pm and a trip costs B150. The ticket is valid for unlimited number of rides, and you can also use it on the regular express boats. A useful commentary is provided on board. This hop-on-and-hop-off service begins at the Sathorn pier and travels upriver to the Phra Athit pier, stopping at eight major piers along the way. Boats leave every 30 minutes.

Cross-river ferries. Bangkok's ferries are used for getting from one side of the river to the other. They cost from B2.5 per journey, and operate from 5am to 10pm or later.

Longtail boat taxis. Bangkok water taxis ply the inner canals, from the centre of town to outlying districts. Tell the conductor your destination when you get on, as boats do not stop otherwise. Tickets cost B5–10; services are roughly every 10 minutes 6am–7pm.

V

VISAS AND ENTRY REQUIREMENTS

For a visit not exceeding 30 days, visitors from many countries, including the UK, Ireland, Canada, Australia, New Zealand, South Africa and the US, do not need a visa to enter Thailand, just a passport valid for at least 6 months, and a return or onward ticket. Visas can usually be extended by up to 30 days at immigration offices throughout the country. If you plan to stay more than a month, obtain a 60-day visa at a Thai consulate or embassy in your country before leaving home. Check www.thaivisa.com or the websites of Thailand's immigration (www.immigration.go.th) and the Ministry of Foreign Affairs (www.mfa.go.th) for details.

W

WEBSITES

www.tourismthailand.org The official site of the Tourism Authority of Thailand with information on all aspects of travel in Thailand.

www.bangkokpost.com The internet version of the daily English-language newspaper is a good site to obtain up-to-the-minute local news and weather reports as well as listings of current cultural events. Its travel archives are an excellent resource on finding discounted hotel and travel packages within Thailand.

www.nationmultimedia.com Daily news from *The Nation* newspaper.

www.phuketgazette.net The website of Phuket's English-language newspaper has news and events related to the island.

www.bangkoktourist.com Information on Bangkok from the Bangkok Tourist Bureau.

www.khaosanroad.com Backpackers' resource with accommodation, work advice, upcountry travel and forums.

Recommended Hotels

Luxury hotels in Bangkok are among the world's least expensive and most travellers take advantage of the many promotional rates offered at the city's world-class establishments. It is imperative to make advance reservations for the high season, from December to March, especially for the resort destinations of Phuket and Ko Samui. During the low season, from April to October, there are almost always rooms to be had. The Tourist Authority of Thailand (TAT) has airport and city-centre offices in all major destinations; many are open seven days a week. All hotels are air-conditioned. A seven percent (from October 2015 10 percent) Value Added Tax (VAT) and 10 percent service charge is added to hotel bills. Unless noted below, all hotels accept major credit cards. Published, or 'rack' rates, may be high at the hotels listed below, but always ask for promotional rates which offer up to 60 percent savings. Reservations made through tour operators or through the TAT will also normally ensure a lower price than the hotel's rack rates. Always check the hotel's website (where available) as many hotels offer 'internet-only' rates, allowing you to make substantial savings.

The following price categories are for accommodation for two people per night, including tax.

$$$$	over US$280
$$$	US$140–280
$$	US$70–140
$	less than US$70

BANGKOK

Arun Residence $$–$$$ *38 Soi Pratoo Nok Yoong, Thanon Maharat, Rattanakosin, tel: 0 2221 9158-9,* www.arunresidence.com. A small riverbank hotel with views of Wat Arun, and just a short walk away from Wat Pho and 100 year-old Chinese shophouses. Rooms have Wi-fi access, DVD players and iPod docks, and there is a French-Thai restaurant, The Deck, and a rooftop bar that makes an atmospheric spot for cocktails. Six rooms.

Intercontinental Bangkok $$$ *973 Ploenchit Road, tel: 0 2656 0444,* www.ihg.com. In the heart of the shopping district, steps from Chit Lom Skytrain station, this hotel is an excellent choice. The deluxe rooms are spacious with large sound-proofed windows overlooking the bustling city. There are five restaurants, a pool, health club, spa and a beauty salon. There's a very cute Italian trattoria and wine bar, called Grossi, on the basement floor. 381 rooms.

The Mandarin Oriental $$$$ *48 Oriental Avenue, tel: 0 2659 9000,* www.mandarin-oriental.com/bangkok. More than 130 years old, the world-renowned Oriental Hotel is Bangkok's longest-established luxury hotel. All the rooms are plush, with special touches such as hardwood floors in the bathrooms. As well as the Oriental Spa, there's a Thai cooking school, seven of the city's best restaurants, two swimming pools and a health club. Afternoon tea is served in the Authors' Lounge, named after the many famous writers who have stayed at the hotel. 395 rooms.

Marvel Hotel $ *30 Sukhumvit Soi 22, Bangkok 10110, tel: 0 2262 0000,* www.marvelhotelbangkok.com. The shopping district of Sukhumvit, including the Emporium shopping complex, is just a few minutes' walk from this well-priced, full-service hotel. Located near Phrom Phong Skytrain station, the rooms come with telephones, satellite television and bathrooms with hairdryers. There's an outdoor swimming pool, a gym, a 24-hour bar and an Italian restaurant. 221 rooms.

Le Méridien $$$–$$$$ *40/5 Surawong Road, tel: 0 2232 8888,* www. lemeridien.com/bangkoksurawong. This new sleek, modernist hotel just 50 metres from Patpong district is a fully wired techno vision of brushed concrete, glass and funky nightclub lighting effects. Rooms have full wall windows, flat screen TVs and 'rainforest' showers. The signature restaurant, Bamboo Chic, fuses Thai, Japanese and Chinese cuisines to a techno soundtrack, and has sake and *shouchu* lists alongside the wine. 282 rooms.

Old Bangkok Inn $$–$$$ *609 Phra Sumen Road, Phra Nakhon, tel: 0 2629 1787,* www.oldbangkokinn.com. A stone's throw from old city historical landmarks, this late 19th-century royal home has teak furniture and fittings. The rooms have satellite TV, DVD players, broadband Internet and even computers. Ten rooms.

The Peninsula $$$$ *333 Charoen Nakhon Road, Khlong San, tel: 0 2861 2888*, www.peninsula.com. This 39-storey luxury hotel has great river views and decor that is international and contemporary but with neat Asian undertones. The marble bathrooms have steam-free TVs, there's an outdoor pool, a health club, and six excellent bars and restaurants, including Mei Jiang, one of the best Chinese in the city. Free shuttle boats to Tha Sathorn pier. 370 rooms.

Shanghai Mansion $$ *479–481 Yaowarat Road, tel: 0 2221 2121*, www.shanghaimansion.com. A classy boutique hotel in a part of town often written off as lacking in any decent lodgings. The artful decor results in accommodation with lovely over-the-top chinoiserie, four-poster beds and vibrant saturated hues, many reflecting those you see in the nearby market alleyways. Also has free internet access, a spa, and free tuk-tuk shuttle to major attractions.

The Swiss Lodge $–$$ *3 Convent Road, Silom, Bangkok 10500, tel: 0 2233 5345*, www.swisslodge.com. A small boutique hotel located near the nightlife and shopping districts, and the Saladaeng Skytrain station. Swiss-managed with friendly, knowledgeable staff. Elegant rooms with teak furniture and marble bathrooms. There's 24-hour room service, a small pool with sundeck and a Swiss café. 55 rooms.

Take a Nap $ *920–926 Rama 4 Road, Suriyawongse, tel: 0 2637 0015*, www. takeanahotel.com. Basic but cutely attired rooms, each with an artistic theme, such as Japanese waves, Pop Art, and the child-like Happy Forest, painted on the wall. They also have air-con and a few TV stations, but no fridge or wardrobe. Close to the Patpong night market and a five-minute walk to the Skytrain and subway stations. 30 rooms.

CHIANG MAI

Chiang Mai Plaza Hotel $ *92 Sridonchai Road, Chang Khlan, tel: 0 5382 0920*. Within walking distance of the Night Bazaar and the Ping

River, this large tourist hotel offers great value. Its spacious public areas are tastefully decorated with Thai art and maintain a relaxed ambience. In the evenings a small Northern Thai music ensemble performs in the main lobby. Facilities include a fitness centre, large outdoor pool and two restaurants serving Thai and international cuisine. Free Wi-fi internet access available. 467 rooms and eight suites.

Dhara Dhevi $$$$ *51/4 Chiang Mai-San Kamphaeng Road, tel: 0 5388 8888, www.dharadhevi.com.* A stunning complex in extensive grounds with villas modelled on local Lanna architecture. In communal areas there are replicas of famous buildings such as the ancient Palace of Mandalay in Burma. Top class restaurants include the French Farang Ses and the Chinese Fujian. 123 suites and villas.

The Four Seasons Resort Chiang Mai $$$$ *502 Moo 1, Mae Rim-Samoeng Old Road tel: 0 5329 8181, www.fourseasons.com/chiang mai.* Thirty minutes from the airport, this world-renowned, lushly landscaped resort hotel overlooks tranquil rice paddies. Accommodation is in two-storey teak pavilions luxuriously furnished with every amenity, including DVD players, internet access and huge bathrooms with deep tubs. These also come with private *sala* (a traditional-style covered verandah) with an oversized day bed and colourful Thai pillows. There's an infinity pool, tennis courts, a spa, a fitness centre and several outstanding restaurants and bars. Shuttle service to the Night Bazaar is provided daily. 98 lodgings, including pavilions, villas and private residencies.

Karinthip Village $–$$$ *50/2 Chang Moi Kao Road, Changmoi Tb. Muang Ap., tel: 0 5323 54 14-8, www.karinthipvillage.com.* Located just outside the old city, Karinthip Village occupies a quiet landscaped corner opposite Wat Chomphu. The three guest wings contain rooms decorated in different themes: Chinese, Thai or colonial. Facilities include a Thai-Western restaurant, large pool and a spa. 67 rooms.

CHIANG RAI

Dusit Island Resort $$–$$$ *1129 Kraisorasit Road, Vieng District, tel: 0 5360 7999, www.dusit.com.* A great hotel located on an island in the Kok river, across from the city centre. Rooms have large picture windows overlooking the city and mountains. There's a large outdoor pool, tennis courts, fitness centre, a steak house, a Chinese restaurant, a steakhouse restaurant, and a Thai café. 271 rooms.

CHIANG SAEN/THE GOLDEN TRIANGLE

Anantara Resort and Spa Golden Triangle $$$$ *229 Moo 1, Chiang Saen tel: 0 5378 4084,* http://goldentriangle.anantara.com. A most unusual low-rise hotel (two-storey buildings) set amid 81 hectares (200 acres) of manicured gardens. The spacious and comfortable rooms with sunken bathrooms all come with a large terrace overlooking the Mekong River, Myanmar and Laos. An elephant camp offers local elephant treks and elephant training lessons. One free activity for every night of stay. 77 rooms and suites.

MAE HONG SON

The Dai $ *158 Toongkongmoo Village, tel: 0 5361 3964,* www.the-dai. com. Owned by a Shan family, The Dai is a lovely property with several Shan-style houses spread across landscaped grounds. The spacious rooms have air conditioning and are warmly decorated with bamboo-thatched walls and wood trim. There is also space in the grounds for camping. 11 rooms.

PHUKET

Amanpuri $$$$ *Pansea Beach, tel: 0 7632 4333,* www.amanpuri. com. The premier property of the exclusive Aman resorts chain has a private beach where every imaginable water sport is available. Perfect for the many movie stars who arrive each year. Pavilions with wood floors and ocean views are scattered on the hillside amid coconut and palm trees. There's also a beautiful pool and the hotel has its own fleet of yachts for day trips or overnight cruises. It has 40 pavilions as well as 30 private villas.

Banyan Tree $$$$ *33 Moo 4 Srisoonthorn Road, Amphoe Talang, 83110, tel: 0 7632 4374,* www.banyantree.com. The epitome of luxury in the midst of a manicured development at Bang Tao Bay. All the villas have wood floors, plush furniture and private outdoor Jacuzzis; some come with private pools, although few overlook the sea. There are free-form and lap pools, tennis courts, water sports, a spa and fitness centre, a golf school and course, cooking classes, and several outstanding restaurants. 108 villas.

Cape Sienna Hotel & Villas $$$–$$$$ *18/40 Moo 6, Nakalay Road, Kamala, Kathu, tel: 0 7633 7300, www.capesienna.com.* Modern accommodation with good views over Kamala Beach. All rooms have sea views, private balconies, flat screen TVs and wireless broadband. Good sea views, too, from its restaurants, bars and spa. This is an adult-friendly resort so only allows children under 12 in family villas, all of which overlook the sea. 146 rooms and nine villas.

Marina Phuket Resort $$$–$$$$ *47 Karon Road, Karon Beach, tel: 0 7633 0625, www.marinaphuket.com.* Small, simply furnished bungalows are scattered on a hillside a few minutes' walk from the sandy beach at Karon. The jungle-like foliage means some rooms remain quite dark throughout the day; the sea view units offer breathtaking scenery to look at. There are two restaurants and a small pool. 104 rooms.

The Royal Phuket Yacht Club $$$$ *23/3 Vises Road, Nai Harn Beach, tel: 0 7638 0200, www.theroyalphuketyachtclub.com.* A lovely hideaway on a cliff above a white-sand beach. Understated luxury in well-equipped rooms that feature oversized terraces with magnificent ocean views. The spa has outdoor treatment rooms overlooking the Andaman Sea and there's a pool, two restaurants and a spa. 110 rooms.

Thavorn Beach Village and Spa $$$ *6/2 Moo 6, Nakalay Bay, Patong, tel: 0 7629 0334, www.thavornbeachvillage.com.* Close to the bustle of Patong, yet tranquil enough with its own private beach. A cable car transports guests from the open-air main lobby to the comfortable rooms built high on a hill. The grounds are lush and service is of a high standard. There's a large lagoon swimming pool, a spa and an excellent Thai restaurant. Contains 194 rooms.

KO SAMUI

Ampha Place Hotel $ *67/59 Moo 1, Thanbol Maenam, tel: 0 7733 2129*, www.samui-ampha-hotel.com. This simple, but well run place has smart ensuite rooms, each with international TV channels, a balcony and free Wi-Fi access. There's a small café and bar beside the outdoor pool. The location is secluded and quiet, about 150 metres/yards to the beach and a ten minute walk into the village of Maenam.

Bo Phut Resort & Spa $$$$ *12/12 Tambol Bo Phut, Surat Thani, tel: 0 7724 5777*, www.bophutresort.com. This 9-hectare (23-acre) luxury resort prides itself on its quiet, restful atmosphere. There's a lovely stretch of private sandy beach with every water sport imaginable. Accommodation is in villas scattered across the grounds, all meticulously decorated with an authentic flair. There's a spa, a glorious pool and three restaurants. 32 Thai-style villas and 29 suites.

Centara Grand Beach Resort $$$$ *38/2 Moo 3, Borpud, Chaweng Beach, tel: 0 7723 0500*, www.centralhotelsresorts.com. This is a large resort hotel in the midst of bustling Chaweng Beach. Rooms are comfortable with their own little private balconies, all with ocean views. There's a fitness centre, spa and three excellent restaurants. 208 rooms.

The Imperial Boat House Beach Resort $$ *83 Moo 5, Choeng Mon Beach, tel: 0 7742 5041*, www.imperialhotels.com/boathouse. This splendid property features comfortable hotel rooms, including 34 rice barge suites with wood floors, luxury bathrooms and amenities. Public areas feature a pool, a beachside restaurant and a bar. 210 rooms.

Poppies Samui $$$ *Chaweng Beach, tel: 0 7742 2419*, www.poppies samui.com. Excellent location at the quieter end of Chaweng Beach, this is a small property with understated luxury in each of its private cottages decorated with fine Thai silk and gleaming teak floors and furniture. The bathrooms feature a sunken bath opening onto a private garden. There's a pool surrounded with natural rock, an outstanding restaurant on the beach and a spa. Consists of 24 cottages.

The Tongsai Bay $$$$ *84 Moo 5, Bo Phut, Tongsai Bay, tel: 0 7724 5480,* www.tongsaibay.co.th. On a quiet bay with a private beach, this hideaway is one of the most luxuriously unpretentious retreats in Thailand. The cottages, scattered on a hillside, all have teak floors, open-air terraces and secluded outdoor tubs. The villas have indoor and outdoor bedrooms (mosquito nets provided), which is an unusual feature for a tropical vacation. It has a mix of 44 cottages, 24 beachfront suites and 15 villas.

HUA HIN

Evason Hua Hin Resort and Spa $$–$$$ *9 Moo 5 Parknampran Beach, Pranburi, Prachuab Khiri Khan, tel: 0 3263 2111,* www.sixsenses.com. Modern elegance situated along an isolated beach with the option of villas that come with their own private pools. The Six Senses Spa offers a range of treatments, including Thai and Himalayan Singing Bowl massage. 240 rooms and suites as well as 40 pool villas.

KO PHI PHI

Holiday Inn Resort Phi Phi Island $–$$ *Laemtong Beach, Phi Phi Island, Krabi, tel: 0 7562 7300,* www.phiphi.holidayinn.com. These bungalows in a smart resort at the remote northerly end of the island have garden or sea views. The resort also has a spa and holds Thai cooking classes in one of its restaurants. Its isolation means tranquillity, though sightseeing is best accomplished by boat. Has 77 bungalows, split between beachfront and garden locations.

INDEX